PRIVATE BANKING
IN EUROPE

'Private banking goes "back to the essential: there is a human being who needs to see a human being who needs to talk things over"'
Patrick Odier
Lombard, Odier

Private banking is one of the highest growth and most profitable financial businesses in Europe. *Private Banking in Europe* provides new insights into this industry. The volume includes:

- a discussion of future prospects and opportunities for private bankers and their clients;
- a debate on the importance of global and local service;
- an analysis of the private banking sector as an embryonic model for change throughout the banking industry;
- a comparison of key players and their chosen markets and strategies – complemented by an exploration of the growth of intermediaries and unexpected competitors;
- a series of interviews with private bankers, showing how they view their industry, their competition and future directions.

The book provides a valuable guide for both students and professionals in the word of private banking.

Lyn Bicker has worked as a technology and business consultant to the financial market in London, mainland Europe and New York since 1987. She is managing director of *The Solutions Organisation*, a consulting firm she founded in 1994; a non-executive director of the East Kent Health Authority; and European co-President of the European Women's Management Development Network.

ROUTLEDGE INTERNATIONAL STUDIES IN MONEY AND BANKING

PRIVATE BANKING IN EUROPE

Lyn Bicker

London and New York

First published 1996
by Routledge
11 New Fetter Lane, London EC4P 4EE

Reprinted 1998, 1999 (twice)

Simultaneously published in the USA and Canada
by Routledge
29 West 35th Street, New York, NY 10001

Routledge is an imprint of the Taylor & Francis Group

© 1996 Lyn Bicker

Typeset in Garamond by Pure Tech India Ltd, Pondicherry
Printed and bound in Great Britain by
Intype London Ltd

British Library Cataloguing in Publication Data
A catalogue record for this book is available from the British Library

Library of Congress Cataloguing in Publication Data
Bicker, Lyn
Private Banking in Europe/Lyn Bicker.
Includes bibliographical references and index.
1. Private banks – Europe. I. Title.
HG2021.E85B53 1996 95–40970

ISBN 0–415–12977–X

CONTENTS

v

CONTENTS

TABLES

EXECUTIVE SUMMARY

There are two main issues facing the private banking sector in the next decade:

- how to take advantage of the tremendous growth potential available in the market;
- how to sustain profitability in the face of increasing competition and fragmentation.

As the polarisation of rich and poor continues, the market for private banking services is expanding – some say at the rate of 10–15 per cent per year. Current market size evaluations suggest there is $9.6 trillion in private wealth worldwide, available wealth of $7.1 trillion and 3.1 million potential customers. Particularly fast growth is being seen in the Asia Pacific region, with Latin America close behind; Europe is key to managing wealth, and demographic changes and cross-generational inheritance of wealth built up since the Second World War will provide accelerating opportunity until the end of the century.

Key to growing private banking business is the recruitment, retention and reward of staff: many other industries may make similar claims, but private banking really does depend on the quality of client-facing staff, their longevity in post and the level of service delivery. Churning of staff does not support the long-term client retention aspirations of the private bank, and finding new ways of motivating individuals when a career path does not appear to exist is a growing problem.

Business levels depend not only on bringing in new clients, but also on 'mining' the current client base, deepening relationships and establishing a bond between banker and client that will survive generations. While market share is built through contacts with professionals, client referral is a major source of new business. Knowledge of the client is becoming more and more important – both from the need to understand what is required, and also to eliminate the possibility of fraudulent or criminal activity, for which the private banker, as agent, may be held responsible.

The redirection of staff towards client-facing and supporting activity is likely to increase, with relationship management teams becoming more prevalent. Specialisation and expertise within the teams is important, as is the ability to reward all team members in a way which supports the bank's business with the client, rather than that of the individual employee.

Profitability of client, service and product can only be sustained through better service for clients, and close attention to their needs. This requires more emphasis on segmentation of the client base, and analysis and measurement of the level of profitability achieved in each segment, ruthlessly weeding out expensive clients where necessary. Differentiation between private banks is poor, and it is difficult for the new client to evaluate or compare offerings; at the same time only part of a client's total wealth is likely to be managed by any one bank, as risk and expectations are spread. As the ability to compare prices improves, there will be greater pressure on value for money, with the subsequent erosion of fees.

Delivery of products demands a diverse approach, and the ability to separate out costs – of research and development, product development, and promotion and delivery. Improvements in time-to-market will be a significant factor as the product lifetime shortens, 'me too' products proliferate, and production becomes simply too expensive unless integration of process across functions is achieved.

At the same time as large, universal banks move more heavily into the private banking market, smaller niche players are also increasing: *gérants de fortune*, independent wealth advisors and substitutes for the sector: insurers, fund managers and managers of fund managers. The sector is becoming increasingly fragmented, as every man and his dog recognises – or assumes – that private banking can be a far more profitable focus than many other banking disciplines. Polarisation between high transaction volume banking – retail, and to a certain extent, trading – and the high value, fee earning services, will continue; smaller and mid-sized players are already turning to institutional services as a way of achieving economy of scale and leveraging business across the two sectors.

The dilemmas facing private banks revolve around choice: choice of bank, choice of relationship and the professional's choice of employer. Change of culture will be a major factor in convincing clients that the private bank they talk to today is the one they wish to continue the conversation with tomorrow. The private banker of the future could be a reinvention of his ancestors: friend, advisor, councellor and, more importantly, entrepreneur. The challenge for banking organisations is to allow such an anomaly to exist.

ACKNOWLEDGEMENTS

I have had a great deal of help and support in the preparation and writing of this book – from many private bankers, their assistants and press officers and I offer them my warmest thanks. I would especially like to thank the following:

Warwick Newbury, at Coutts & Co.; Michael Burmester, at Coutts International; Cliff Slater, at Bank Julius Baer; Rod Hearne and Ivan Pictet, at Pictet et Cie; Thierry Lombard and Patrick Odier at Lombard, Odier et Cie; Werner Peyer, at Crédit Suisse; Georges Vergnion, at Chase Manhattan; Hap Russell and René Boehrer at Citibank; Urs Eberhardt at Swiss Bank Corporation; Jim Chibbett and Catherine McDowell at Barclays; Lucy Rinaldi, at Bankers Trust; Peter Braunwalder at UBS; Charles Ruppert and Lucien Theal, at the Association des Banques et Banquiers, Luxembourg; Michel Dérobert of the Genevan Association des Banques Privées; Catherine Sweet, at the British Bankers Association; Utz Pfannschmidt, at Hardy & Co Privatbankiers; Richard Moseley, at HSBC; Jacques de Watteville at the Swiss Embassy; and many others.

My family, as ever, have been my greatest support; special thanks also go to Alison Dickens, who managed to turn my scribble into typescript, and to Leslie Gardner, my agent. With all their support, perhaps one day I too will be a private banker's dream client!

Kent, 1995

1

INTRODUCTION

To start at the beginning: what is private banking? Definitions abound: the provision of wealth management services; wealth protection for the high net worth individual (HINWI); the offering of investment services and products to support wealthy individuals' needs. Most people in the banking sector understand that private banking is at the far end of the scale from retail banking; it is something which rich people will happily pay for, in the expectation that they will preserve and possibly increase their fortune.

Some definitions of private banking show a growing reliance and emphasis on private banking 'products', an approach carried over from the mass market and the corporate sector, both of which are transaction-oriented. This is one thing that private banking is not.

In truth, private banking is any service the client wants it to be. Be it wealth management, money transmission, portfolio management, the delivery of a yacht or walking the dog, private banking is the ultimate client-led business.

Originating in the mercantile economies of the Renaissance, private banking is the oldest manifestation of money management. When the Dutch republic accepted the validity of trade and commerce, it also established the basic needs of its traders, those successful progenitors of modern business. They required a bridge between trade and finance – ways of keeping their family fortune safe, of raising loans, of investing wisely. Through the centuries, wealthy folk turned to bankers for help not only in managing their affairs, but also in exploiting the commercial value of their inherited land.

With industrialisation came a greater need for finance capital, and many of the Swiss private banks originated as houses organising the financing of infrastructural labour. The Genevan banks identified an early need to specialise, and went for the top end of the market as deposit banks – looking after their private clients.

During the twentieth century, political and ideological developments, and the increasing efficiency of instruments of destruction during the two world wars, created enormous growth in the need for lending. Banks grew, as did

1

their bureaucracy; the man in the street needed volume transactions, which appeared to be the most profitable business focus. Many banks lost interest in the wealthy and the highly individualised service they required.

The complexity of modern life drove the need for specialist advice more and more, and private banks with their concentration on taking deposits from wealthy individuals and families and managing their investments – for a fee – built successful and profitable businesses. So profitable, in fact, that in the less happy days of the early and late 1980s, their sister banks woke up to the fact that this was a sector where good return on capital could be expected. Extremely good, in fact.

Over the last 15 years, it seems that every man and his dog see private banking as the place to be. Competition has increased, with traditional banks jostling for business alongside global universal banks, and with niche players moving smartly around the big boys' ankles to create their own success.

Today, the private banking market is growing, but so is the number of interested parties. Pressures on costs and margins are increasing, and as clients become more knowledgeable they expect ever-greater absolute performance. They would like pricing transparency, too, a concept private bankers prefer not to move into.

The capital requirements of private banking are not high, although any diversion of capital into off-balance-sheet activities has an impact on capital adequacy ratios. The human capital investment is much higher: a service-led business delivered to demanding clients needs highly professional practitioners, and to provide them with adequate and ideally leading-edge tools to do their job. Bankers agree that 'we're all in the relationship business', and high quality relationship management is a prerequisite for success. More than many other sectors, private banking is also a knowledge business. It depends both on 'who' and 'what' the private banker knows.

As the world becomes a small place by virtue of communications media and infrastructure, the established private bank faces new competition from 'disintermediaries': clever constructions of investment management and advice which get in the way of the relationship between client and banker. While the sector relies on its traditionally staid, comfortable and secure image, it is becoming as affected by rationalisation and fragmentation as other industries, and must consider flavours of advanced management thought in order to provide future profits. Private banking is an activity that relies on long-term thinking.

MARKET ATTRACTIVENESS

One problem presented by a growing and attractive market is its very attractiveness. Seen as rich pickings for many varieties of banker and financial services provider, the market has produced a proliferation of new players. The return on capital is high, although entry barriers are also considerable: plush premises, expensive and high quality people, and superb information technology capability are minimum requirements. Add in an international presence, and the associated telecommunications, and it is clear that getting into private banking is not something to be taken lightly. Once in, the player has to be there for the long term. Cost of customer acquisition is high, with a norm of 'revenue-neutral' for the first year of the relationship. Since the whole thrust of private client services is towards a long-term and ever-deeper relationship with the client, perhaps spanning generations as well as a variety of family branches, it is not an undertaking for those merely seeking a quick profit.

For those prepared to stay, however, private banking is a lucrative if highly competitive business. Most activity is off-balance-sheet, and therefore does not use massive capital after the initial investment; almost all income is fee-based, and the charges in the industry range between 0.8 and 1.5 per cent of assets managed.

With that kind of return on a repeat fee basis, it is little wonder that the big banks see private banking as a profitable diversion. Global reach, established telecommunications and information technology, significant existing investment in trading and portfolio analysis capability: all these factors mean that they already have many of the necessary ingredients for success in the private banking market.

MARKET PRESSURES

The *established players* trade on their reputation, history and connections. With pedigrees of two or three hundred years, a number of the traditional Swiss private banks, for example, have long been the *confidantes* of the rich and influential, and maintain their solid reputation assiduously. Secrecy, or at least confidentiality, is another key factor, not solely for protection from legal and fiscal requirements, but often simply to maintain protection from the prying eyes of others. Of course if you are a HINWI – a high net worth individual – you want to remain so, and therefore the reputation of your financial advisor is crucial. So is the image, which is clearly portrayed by the attention to very smart buildings, antique furniture and original works of art. Most private banks gain a high percentage of new customers via referral, which means that 'connections' are extremely important.

Global, or at least international, reach is another plus for those established in private banking. Apart from being in touch with their clients as and when needed, presence in the major financial centres is essential. Of equal importance is influence within that community, whether as holder of a stock exchange seat or leader of a banking committee addressing a specific issue. Relationship between client and advisor is of course based on service, and benefits mightily from the perception of peer-to-peer value.

For prospective *new entrants*, entry barriers also include the requirement for a long-term strategy, largely service-led. Some of the newer players have driven their gains in market share by the creation of a range of products not apparently available, or with such good performance, from their competitors. Their 'new ideas' attract investors with a greater degree of tolerance of risk; younger HINWIs have studied at major universities and business schools; entrepreneurs are often well versed in the possibilities of portfolio management, if not experienced, and the general increase in available, published advice and information for investors, on an almost daily basis, has its own effect in raising financial awareness.

Getting out of the sphere of private banking has almost as many barriers as getting in. Quick profit takers need not apply: profits are long term, depend on stability, trust and development of the client–advisor relationship, and pulling out does not augur well for any future attempt to get back into the market. Private banking can also create demand for other 'full-service' provision: Citibank's credit exposure risk analysis service, for example, has application for businesses owned by the HINWI, as well as the investment portfolio.

The profitability of the business continues to attract *substitutes* to the market, though. These include fund managers; lawyers, accountants and other professionals; traditional stockbrokers and investment management houses; and a range of products which can be picked off the shelf. It is in this area of substitution that the market for private clients begins to be more segmented: movement down the scale shows far more product-orientation, with a dash of service. The listings of fund movements in the *Financial Times* illustrate the variety and number on offer, a high proportion of which are sold through direct mail or advertisement.

A fairly recent development has been the 'fund of funds', and manager of managers (see Chapter 8), although memories are long in this business, and scandals of 20 or 30 years ago still serve as a gating factor for some of these products.

Linked to growing sophistication and expectation among clients is a degree of self-financial-management, too. It is accepted by banking professionals that clients are not likely to put all their eggs in one basket any more. By spreading their investment portfolios, they of course increase the competition between service providers, but as at least one banker says, 'We hope to attract clients by one of our core products and then bring them completely into the fold.'

2

THE PRIVATE BANKING MARKET

The market for private banking services has been described as one which 'will take care of itself'. What private banking provides is a service, as defined by customer requirements; as the world continues to polarise between rich and poor, it is clear that more people are indeed becoming wealthy, and are therefore open to private banking services. The scope of the market is, however, extremely difficult to bound, and to size:

- it is global, though needing local focus;
- it services wealthy individuals who may range from 'thousandaires' to billionaires;
- its client base is made up of individuals who are generally reticent in admitting the extent of their wealth;
- clients have a range of differing requirements as a result of their position in the wealth lifecyle, and the environment in which they live.

This presents a problem not seen in other banking areas: identification of the size of the market. Every private bank will agree that the market is huge. Citibank figures in 1988 suggested that available assets amounted to $7.1 trillion, spread among some 3.1 million potential customers. Research by Chase Manhattan Private Bank in 1993 estimated that private wealth worldwide totalled more than $9.6 trillion, an increase of 35 per cent in five years, while McKinsey's figures suggested a private banking market size of $2 trillion in January 1991.

Establishing the location of the market as well as its size is also problematic. Countries in the Pacific rim, agreed by most economic commentators to be the engine of growth, are certainly producing growing numbers of HINWIs. The ABN-Amro Bank estimates that the size of the private banking market in Asia, excluding Japan, is $400–500 billion.

Chase's research indicates that around six million individuals worldwide have disposable assets of more than $250,000. Of these, probably a third maintain their financial assets offshore.[1] Around 2.6 million of these have liquid – i.e. available for investment – assets in excess of $1 million, and half a million of them use offshore facilities to maintain their financial assets.

5

Chase suggest that $2.1 trillion is invested offshore, with $7.5 trillion invested locally with domestic institutions, through local and multicurrency services provided to the investor by a locally based institution.[2] In Europe, it is thought that seven million individuals are potential private banking clients.

INTERNATIONAL COMPARISONS: CLIENT POTENTIAL FOR PRIVATE BANKERS

American Express estimates of very high net worth individuals in 1989 are shown in Table 2.1.

Table 2.1 Clients over $10 million net worth

Country	No.	Ratio
UK	8,000	1 in 7,125
Italy	9,500	1 in 6,105
Mexico	3,000	1 in 29,333
Venezuela	760	1 in 26,316
India	3,400	1 in 250,000
Indonesia	900	1 in 200,000
USA	49,600	1 in 5,060

Source: IBC conference 'Success in Private Banking', 1992

Based on an accumulation of data from tax authorities and published sources, the potential is astonishingly high. However, ABN-Amro's 1994 assessment of the numbers of high net worth individuals in Asia Pacific is rather different, as shown in Table 2.2.

Table 2.2 HINWIs in Asia Pacific region, 1994 estimate

Country	No. of HINWIs
Indonesia	18,000
Philippines	Under 12,000
Southern China	Negligible
Taiwan	61,000
Thailand	17,000
Malaysia	Under 15,000

Source: ABN-Amro Bank, 1994

Levels of net worth here are undefined, which may account for the apparent twentyfold increase in Indonesia over five years. However, it is certainly true that wealth is being accumulated very quickly in the region. Chase

6

Manhattan's research suggests that wealthy individuals are concentrated in the following countries: USA, Brazil, India, Italy, Japan, Mexico, Argentina, Germany, South Korea, Spain, Israel, South Africa, France, Indonesia, Thailand, Greece, Hong Kong, Chile, UK, Switzerland, Turkey, Saudi Arabia, Venezuela and Kuwait.

The number of high net worth individuals with an annual asset income of more than $1m is compared by region in Table 2.3. In the United States there are more than two million households with an asset income in excess of $1m per annum. The total assets held by these households is estimated to be $4,165,000m. In Europe, the Middle East and Africa, there are a total of 250,000 households with asset income of more than $1m. Total net assets are worth an estimated $635,000m.

Table 2.3 Number of households with annual asset income of more than $1m

Country	Thousands of households	US $ thousand million
USA	2,090	4,165
Western Hemisphere	250	635
Europe/Middle East/Africa	415	1,735
Asia Pacific	380	630
World total	3,135	7,165

Source: Citibank, 1992

The USA accounts for 66.7 per cent of households with asset income of more than $1m but only 58.1 per cent of the assets. The highest concentration of assets to households ratio occurs in the Europe/Middle East/Africa region. The Middle East is primarily responsible for this weighting.

Table 2.4 Household/asset distribution by region, 1991

Country	% Households with income > $1m	% Assets
USA	66.7	58.1
Western Hemisphere	8.0	8.9
Europe/Middle East/Africa	13.2	24.2
Asia Pacific	12.1	8.8
World total	100.0	100.0

Source: Datamonitor/Citibank, 1992

THE EUROPEAN PICTURE: EQUALLY CONFUSED

In Europe, Germany heads the league table for the most mid to high net worth individuals, estimated in 1991 at 46 per cent. Switzerland, France,

Spain, Belgium and the UK come lower down the rankings. In the UK, the Inland Revenue estimates that 750,000 people have an annual income in excess of £50,000. This seems a conservative figure, based on employment rather than entrepreneurial activity, but still represents 1.6 per cent of the adult population. Kleinwort Benson estimates that in fact 9 per cent of European households with an income of £85,000 are UK-based. Lloyds Private Bank have yet another set of figures, as shown in Table 2.5.

Table 2.5 UK private banking market 1985–92: figures in thousands

Asset values over	1985	1987	1988	1990	1992 (estimated)
£50,000	573	725	1,038	1,225	1,400
£100,000	218	295	373	489	575
£250,000	335	424	600	698	820
£500,000	12	25	26	45	53

Source: Lloyds Private Bank, 1993

A more fruitful comparison for identifying client potential is to consider the savings habits of each country.

The UK

Financial assets in the UK are usually fixed, i.e. housing, and the GDP *per capita* is the second lowest in Europe. The most popular investment vehicles are savings and stocks/shares; in 1989 around 30 per cent of the population owned some form of financial product. Most investments are bought through banks, building societies or institutions, a highly competitive market. Britons are generally risk-averse, with an inclination to try to save.

A key segment of the UK private client market is that of expatriates. Some will return to the UK, either as employees or to retire, and can represent an important area for new business. There are approximately five million UK expats, three million of whom have been working abroad for 20 years. A high proportion – 47 per cent – work in the European Union; 25 per cent have a senior management role, and 60 per cent are aged between 25 and 50. Their average salary is £35–50k, and 50 per cent have financial assets of more than £100k. This increases to 80 per cent when property is included. The average expat claims ownership of assets valued at £400k; the group invests heavily, saving more than £10k per year.[3]

In 1991, 43 per cent invested in stocks and shares, 29 per cent in offshore funds and bank accounts. A lower percentage invest in unit trusts and pensions, although in 1991 there was a 3 per cent growth in this area. Most UK expats get their investment advice via specialist magazines and newspapers; there appears to be growth in the financial intermediary market for expats.

Inland Revenue figures for 1991 estimated that there were 442,910 individuals in the UK with a net worth of more than £300,000, a 100 per cent growth from 1986. Clearly the boom years of the late 1980s generated much of this growth in wealth; in addition the general ageing of the population, and the greater degree of wealth being released through the death of property owning relatives has had a significant impact. Segmentation by asset shows an interesting picture: in 1991, for example, individuals with a net worth of more than £2m held 85.7 per cent of UK government and municipal securities, and 42.9 per cent of overseas and foreign securities.

Table 2.6 UK high net worth individuals: wealth concentration by asset, 1991

Range of net capital	%	%	%	%	%
Value of estate (lower limit) in £k	UK govt and municipal securities	Overseas and foreign securities	Unlisted company securities	Listed company securities incl. unit trusts	Cash, incl. bank and interest bearing accounts
300	61.5	8.2	22.1	65.4	94.2
500	64.5	13.2	36.8	77.6	94.7
1,000	60.0	20.0	53.3	86.7	100.0
2,000	85.7	42.9	57.1	100.0	100.0
	Loans/ mortgages	Insurance policies	Household goods	Shares in partnership	Trade assets and other personal
300	4.8	64.9	95.7	17.8	52.9
500	7.9	63.2	98.7	22.4	55.3
1,000	20.0	46.7	100.0	20.0	60.0
2,000	14.3	71.4	100.0	28.6	85.7
	UK residential buildings	Other UK buildings	UK land	Foreign immovables	
300	84.1	6.7	14.4	3.4	
500	92.1	9.2	17.1	7.9	
1,000	73.3	6.7	26.7	6.7	
2,000	100.0	14.3	28.6	14.3	

Source: Datamonitor/Inland Revenue, 1991

Germany

The growth of wealth in Germany is summarised by Hardy & Co. Privatbankiers, part of the Dresdner Bank, thus:

Consider the dynamic change which has taken place in Germany's economic environment in latter post-war years. The situation is characterised by a strong increase in personal fortunes. The Germans have meanwhile accumulated assets worth over DM7 trillion. Even if a significant proportion is tied up in private real estate, they already had monetary assets worth more than DM3,400 billion at their disposal by the end of 1991, according to statistics from the Bundesbank. Over DM220 billion are added to this every year.[4]

In general, the German preference is for bonds rather than stocks/shares, and for financial assets rather than fixed assets. Around 42 per cent of people owned some form of financial product in 1991, with unit trust holders aged 25–44, a rather younger profile than other European countries. The savings ratio is very steady, and compares well with France.

During the early 1990s the German investment income account deteriorated dramatically. After record surpluses amounting to about DM30bn at the beginning of the decade, net investment income was halved to DM15bn

Table 2.7 Sight and time deposits of domestic individuals in Germany

DMbn	Total	Sight deposits Self-employed	Employees	Others
1991	239.5	52.5	162.3	24.6
1992	273.5	58.8	183.8	30.8
1993	310.3	67.7	203.7	38.8
1994	315.0	65.5	210.2	39.3

DMbn	Total	Time deposits Self-employed	Employees	Other
1991	339.0	99.0	192.4	47.6
1992	386.4	104.6	226.3	n/a
1993	436.1	115.7	256.2	n/a
1994	361.0	97.4	210.8	n/a

Source: Deutsche Bundesbank Monthly Reports/Business Interventions, 1994

Table 2.8 Savings deposits in Germany

DMbn	Total	Of residents	At 3 months	At 3 months +	Of non-residents
1990	765.04	729.5			9.8
1991	764.8	731.1			10.7
1992	785.0	770.7	522.2	248.6	14.2
1993	877.2	859.4	587.4	272.0	17.7
1994	959.3	940.4	654.3	286.1	

Source: Deutsche Bundesbank Monthly Reports/Business Interventions, 1994

by 1993, and went into an estimated deficit of approximately DM10bn in 1994.

The explanation for this phenomenon largely lies with the German tax laws. Where residents had transferred their safe custody accounts abroad for tax reasons, or had purchased domestic securities through foreign financial centres, and had left them there for safe-keeping, the interest which they earn and which is paid to the bank carrying the safe custody account is reported as investment income payments to non-residents. Corresponding interest credited by the foreign custodian bank to the resident holder of the safe custody account is not recorded. (Note: the effect of German tax legislation changes on private banking in Luxembourg is discussed in the section on Luxembourg, on p. 58.)

At the same time, there has been an above average rise in interest payments on securities, which have gone up fourfold since 1990 and now account for the lion's share of Germany's investment income expenditure. Bonds held by German banks for resident private investors fell in 1993 by DM22bn.

France

The French GDP *per capita* has been growing steadily, and influences the relatively high and stable savings ratio. Savings, stocks and shares are the most popular investment vehicles, with a very high 83 per cent of the population owning a financial product in some form. The French are not averse to debt; they purchase their financial products through a bank or building society. A great deal of French investment has gone into the SICAV (Collective Investment Companies with Variable Capital) over the years since the Second World War.

Table 2.9 Les actifs monétaires détenus par des non-résidents

FFmilliards	1988	1989	1990	1991	1992
Dépôts à vue	34.3	43.0	47.1	45.4	47.8
Livrets soumis à l'impôt	3.1	3.4	3.5	3.7	3.8
Comptes d'épargnelogement	0.3	0.3	0.3	0.4	0.4
Dépôts à terme	105.8	115.8	142.0	181.4	206.9
Titres de créances négociables	39.0	90.2	172.8	212.8	265.4
en francs	34.2	82.8	161.4	199.2	237.7
bons du trésor	27.4	69.8	132.1	157.0	198.6
certs. de dépôt	6.8	13.0	27.8	40.4	36.1
bons des ISF	—	—	1.6	1.8	3.1
Bons de caisse et d'épargne	1.7	2.5	2.2	1.1	0.3
Plan d'épargnelogement	1.1	1.3	1.4	1.5	1.9

Source: *Annuaire Statistique de la France*; Banque de France; Business Interventions, 1994

Table 2.10 Les actifs monétaires en dévises étrangères détenus par des agents non financiers résidents

Situation en fin d'année	Milliards de Francs				
	1988	1989	1990	1991	1992
Dépôts à vue	22.6	24.9	25.5	31.6	34.4
dont lesquels					
Sociétiés	9.4	13.4	15.9	21.5	22.4
Ménages	0.7	0.7	1.0	1.2	1.6
Autres agents	4.1	4.8	4.3	4.7	5.3
Non repartis	8.4	5.9	4.3	4.1	5.0
Dépôts à terme	17.6	37.9	33.5	33.1	28.5
dont lesquels					
Sociétiés	13.9	31.8	25.7	25.4	20.3
Ménages	0.9	1.5	2.8	4.0	4.6
Autres agents	2.8	4.7	4.9	3.6	3.7
Non repartis	—	—	—	—	—
Titres de créances négociables	18.0	29.8	3.2	0.1	0.7
Bons de caisse on d'épargne	—	—	—	—	—

Source: *Annuaire Statistique de la France*; Banque de France; Business Interventions, 1994

Italy

The Italians have the highest European savings ratio, and prefer financial assets to fixed assets. Their GDP *per capita* grew very quickly in the 1980s; 18 per cent of the population own some form of financial product, with bonds and savings as the most popular investment form. Unit trust sales have plummeted since 1985; most products are bought through banks and building societies, but with some through brokers and insurance companies.

The turbulent investment and government environment in Italy is having a considerable effect on its wealthy individuals, and a number of the larger private banks have either opened offices in the country or are actively seeking to gain Italian clients.

Italian portfolio investment abroad fluctuated, particularly during 1993. Italian residents did not switch wholesale into foreign currency assets in response to the narrowing of interest rate differentials between the lira and the major currencies, unlike foreign investors. In fact there was a net capital inflow of L3.5 trillion in the first half of the year. However, direct foreign investment by Italian residents resulted in a net outflow of L7.6 trillion, compared with L2.2 trillion in the previous six months.

Table 2.11 Capital movements: net flows in billions of lire

Year	1992				1993	
	Q1	Q2	Q3	Q4	Q1	Q2
Non-bank capital flows	−13,521	−16,051	−12,207	−15,322	30,059	25,238	8,942
Foreign investment in Italy	16,683	1,218	6,485	−224	9,204	24,559	24,998
of which: portfolio	*12,788*	*811*	*4,954*	*−506*	*7,529*	*23,268*	*23,836*
Italian investment abroad	−31,490	−22,740	−18,646	−15,490	25,386	−1,656	−2,484
of which: portfolio	*−24,152*	*−20,750*	*−15,495*	*−14,267*	*26,360*	*3,521*	*−40*
Foreign loans	9,076	7,639	278	2,499	−1,340	5,435	−1,488
Italian loans	−5,882	−797	−1,987	−1,308	−1,790	−256	−2,848
Trade credits, other capital movements	−1,908	−1,371	1,663	−799	−1,401	−2,844	−9,236
Bank capital flows	25,303	23,284	18,356	−17,214	877	−13,480	−15,445

Source: Bank of Italy Economic Bulletin, October 1993

The Bank of Italy saw a 13.2 per cent reduction in the surplus of the household sector's financial balance in the first half of 1993, and ascribed it to a sharp slowdown in household savings. Interest rates were declining,

Table 2.12 Financial assets and liabilities in billions of lire

	Households			
	Flows			Stocks
	1992 H1	1992 H2	1993 H1	Dec. 1992
Cash	−2,394	10,795	−3,456	77,483
Transferable sight deposits	−22,606	21,805	−19,645	331,329
Other deposits	9,995	35,916	18,665	553,788
Short-term securities	15,733	41,821	2,808	351,007
Medium- and long-term securities	31,505	−1,166	34,489	502,819
Government	*24,184*	*462*	*19,832*	*418,092*
Investment fund units	5,068	−4,336	6,313	60,663
Shares and participations	3,912	2,618	9,552	545,422
External assets	14,765	−7,349	−3,090	84,825
Other	20,291	19,665	15,599	255,168
Total assets	76,226	119,769	61,205	2,762,504
Short-term loans	5,555	1,671	1,090	117,833
Banks	*5,147*	*1,929*	*1,275*	*113,130*
Medium- and long-term loans	8,458	3,058	3,835	165,988
Banks	*4,623*	*165*	*1,381*	*71,320*
Special credit institutions	*4,079*	*3,143*	*2,708*	*77,000*
Other	3,793	4,481	5,570	68,137
Total liabilities	17,806	9,210	10,495	351,958
Balance	58,420	110,559	50,710	—

Source: Bank of Italy Economic Bulletin, October 1993

and short-term securities accounted for a very small share of the L37.2 trillion of net securities acquisitions. Investment in shares, capital parts and investment fund units, however, was more than 70 per cent up on the corresponding period in 1992. Households' overall demand for credit contracted from around L18 trillion in the first half of 1992 to L10.5 trillion.

Real disposable incomes and income expectations have been affected by the increase in the tax burden, the fall in employment and the rise in the cost of imports as a result of the depreciation of the lira. Fears of a collapse in the financial markets became widespread in the autumn of 1992, and a growing proportion of savings was transferred abroad. The contraction in saving in both real and nominal terms is mirrored in reduced financial investment by households, which have disposed of some of the assets they had previously accumulated.

Netherlands

Surprisingly, the Netherlands has a very low savings ratio, with a GDP *per capita* similar to Italy. Financial products are owned by 10 per cent of the population, with pension funds and post office savings forming the most popular instruments. Bonds are more popular than shares, which are purchased mainly through banks and building societies. The number of millionaires is growing, and they seem to be getting younger; Graninger heads the league table of regional affluence.

Scandinavia

During 1985–90, Scandinavia in general had high average wage rate increases, and Sweden had the highest GDP *per capita* in Europe in 1991. Swedes prefer stocks/shares and bonds, with shares leading the ranks, and this is also the case in Denmark. In Norway, by contrast, pension funds are the most popular form of investment.

Table 2.13 Income and taxes in Scandinavia, 1992: units of national currency in millions

	Denmark	Finland	Iceland	Norway	Sweden
Number of income earners	4.38	4.10	0.18	3.18	8.09
Gross taxable income	673,011	335,778	227,347	362,547	966,599
Taxes on income and net wealth	218,614	96,912	32,883	121,350	274,658
Taxes on income and net wealth as % of taxable income	32	29	12	33	28

Source: Nordic Statistics Secretariat/Business Interventions, 1992

Table 2.14 Scandinavian national income and national disposable income, 1989–93: units of national currency in millions

		Compensation of employees	Indirect taxes	Total national disposable income
Denmark	1989	422,094	140,201	660,835
	1990	439,262	141,523	687,955
	1991	452,933	144,462	710,117
	1992	468,410	148,593	733,666
	1993	473,890	153,351	753,965
Finland	1989	264,582	75,595	399,605
	1990	288,768	78,025	417,177
	1991	289,775	74,730	385,134
	1992	273,616	71,643	366,238
	1993	262,231	71,556	363,897
Iceland	1989	153,392	72,152	259,565
	1990	173,696	79,162	307,257
	1991	200,380	83,965	335,131
	1992	203,000	83,763	334,737
	1993	204,800	78,690	343,528
Norway	1989	328,600	36,599	499,083
	1990	342,003	39,992	535,676
	1991	356,381	42,770	556,892
	1992	368,476	44,395	565,591
	1993	373,161	49,149	591,929
Sweden	1989	756,614	55,719	1,031,935
	1990	851,189	63,268	1,126,487
	1991	895,127	72,710	1,202,860
	1992	883,597	78,634	1,180,068
	1993	858,021	81,299	1,170,480

Source: Nordic Statistics Secretariat/Business Interventions

Table 2.15 Savings ratio trends in Europe, 1985–9

Country	1985	1986	1987	1988	1989
Italy	17.75	15.80	14.00	13.50	13.00
France	14.00	13.00	11.25	11.90	12.00
Germany	11.25	12.00	12.50	13.00	12.50
UK	9.50	8.00	6.00	5.50	6.00
Netherlands	2.00	2.50	2.00	2.30	1.50

Source: Kleinwort Benson, 1991
Note: net household savings as percentage of disposable household income. UK figures based on gross savings

Table 2.16 Investment purchases, 1990: buying channels

Country	Institution	% Shares	% Unit Trusts
Germany	Bank/building society	72.0	49.0
	Broker	10.0	11.0
	Advert	2.0	2.0
	Other	16.0	38.0
Italy	Bank/building society	59.0	41.0
	Broker	18.0	10.0
	Insurance company rep.	15.0	8.0
	Advert	3.0	—
	Other	5.0	41.0
UK	Bank/building society	37.0	19.0
	Broker	14.0	26.0
	Insurance company rep.	4.0	17.0
	Advert	16.0	14.0
	Other	29.0	24.0
Netherlands	Bank/building society	62.0	59.0
	Broker	4.0	9.0
	Insurance company rep.	30.0	26.0
	Advert	n/a	4.0
France	Bank/building society	52.0	50.0
	Broker	2.0	—
	Insurance company rep.	1.0	4.0
	Other	45.0	46.0

Source: Kleinwort Benson, 1991

MARKET SEGMENTATION

Segmentation of available clients can be both by degree of wealth and attitude to wealth. Some categories found useful by the bigger banks are as follows:

- Active investors with a net worth exceeding $10m. This sector, which is not geographically defined, can be subdivided into:
  - those seeking to build their wealth, perhaps in the early stages of building their fortune, highly entrepreneurial and willing to take on a high level of risk to achieve their goals;
  - more mature investors who have built their net worth to the point where they actively manage a complex portfolio of direct and indirect investments;
  - extremely wealthy individuals, often having personal staff to assist in the business management of a wide-ranging portfolio;
  - rather older investors, who are reducing their level of active involvement in business investments with a large cash position as a result.

- Professionals – lawyers, accountants, etc. – with partnership or potential partnership status.
- Affluent households and individuals in targeted geographies. Likely to have between $1m and $10m available for investment, they can be further segmented:

  - risk-averse: these may represent 25 per cent of the market, with requirement for relationship consolidation, orchestration and personal help. They probably have low confidence in their own investment ability, and shun risk. They seek and value high level service, and are not price-sensitive;
  - risk-tolerant: probably 12–15 per cent of market. These clients like relationship management and personal help; they are willing to take risks and are relatively insensitive to price and return;
  - self-confident: around 20 per cent of the market. No value is perceived in financial orchestration by this segment, who need little personal help, and are confident of their own investment decision-making ability. Willing to take risks, they are least price- and return-sensitive.

- Established entrepreneurs: wealthy individuals in the 'tiger' and developing economies requiring investment diversification. Their likely focus is Hong Kong, Australia, the Philippines, Japan.
- Energising entrepreneurs: individuals building wealth through continued investment in local business and management of private investment portfolios. They may develop diversification of both business and family investments; likely focus is Taiwan, Korea, Thailand, Indonesia, and Singapore.

SOURCES OF GROWTH: WHERE IS THE POTENTIAL?

Forecasts for growth are hard to validate, or even imagine; what is clear is that the market is growing steadily, and senior bankers forecast a 10–15 per cent a year further growth over the next 5–10 years. Some even go further, as the figures from the 1993 Price Waterhouse *European Private Banking Survey* show (see Table 2.17). Working on a 10 per cent compound annual growth rate, if the market today is worth $9.6 trillion, by the end of the century it could have grown to an astonishing $17 trillion. Germany, Switzerland and Luxembourg are areas which expect particular growth; Price Waterhouse's figures show only 1 in 20 private bankers surveyed believing that growth would be less than 5 per cent.

Table 2.17 Growth potential: optimism in the private banking market

% Responses	Assessment of growth per year in next five years (%)
Less than 5	0–5
20–25	5–10
45–50	10–15
15–20	15–20
5–10	More than 20
5–10	Not known

Source: Price Waterhouse, 1993

Contrary to the wisdom of the old proverb, it is actually the rich who are always with us: wealthy individuals and families who have been rich for a considerable period of time, and who are frequently connected by family and marriage. While their wealth grows, their numbers may not.

The *nouveau riche*, however, do grow in number. They come in many varieties: the post-war generation who have inherited property or other assets slowly built up by parents; the entrepreneurs who have also built up both business and personal assets over a medium term; the highly successful professional investors who have shared in substantial gains and bonuses from their companies but legally are bound to place their own investments elsewhere; high flying company executives; and, of course, those in the world of media and entertainment.

Rapid growth is being seen in both Asia Pacific and Latin America, with available assets of $0.65 trillion and $0.35 trillion respectively, according to Chase; $1 trillion is assessed as available in Europe and the Middle East, with $0.1 trillion as 'other'. The wealth of the Middle East continues to attract attention, although it does appear to have lost some of its lustre, as the market becomes more mature.

Some newly industrialised countries have seen far higher growth rates than those in Europe for some time, with much entrepreneurial activity and associated wealth.

Table 2.18 Average annual growth, 1985–92

Region	GDP(%)	GDP per person(%)
Asia	7.0	5.0
Middle East and Europe	3.9	0.8
Latin America	2.1	0.2
Africa	2.0	(0.4)
Eastern Europe and former Soviet Union	(2.5)	(3.8)
OECD	2.5	2.0

Source: World Bank/IMF

Table 2.19 World GDP at purchasing power parity, 1990

Developing countries		34.4
of which	China	6.3
	Other	28.1
Eastern Europe and former Soviet Union		11.2
Developed countries		54.4
of which	US	22.5
	Japan	7.6
	Other	24.3

Source: IMF/*The Economist*

With a tradition of personal saving, average incomes per head in the Asia Pacific area are a match for the bottom of the Western European league table. A high level of fixed capital investment, financed mainly by high

Table 2.20 GDP per person in emerging markets: $k at purchasing power parity

1992 estimates	
India	1.2
China	2.0
Philippines	2.1
Indonesia	2.5
Thailand	6.0
Malaysia	8.0
South Korea	9.0
Taiwan	14.1
Singapore	16.0
Hong Kong	19.6
Poland	5.0
Russia	6.0
Hungary	6.0
Former Czechoslovakia	6.0
South Africa	5.2
Turkey	5.2
Greece	8.2
Portugal	10.0
Israel	14.0
Argentina	5.2
Brazil	5.5
Mexico	7.5
Chile	7.5
Venezuela	8.2
OECD	17.5

Source: World Bank/*The Economist*, 1992

domestic savings, is part of the secret behind the rapid growth of Asian economies. Investment in Asian developing countries has risen from an average of 27 per cent of GDP in the second half of the 1970s, to 31 per cent so far in the 1990s. By contrast, in Latin America, the share of investment in GDP has fallen from 24 per cent to 20 per cent over the same period.[5]

As can be seen in Table 2.20, the GDP per head in Hong Kong is US$19,600, higher than the average of OECD countries; by contrast India's figure is only $1,200 per head. Clearly, this has considerable impact on the available number of high net worth individuals in particular countries.

THE PRIVATE BANKER'S PROBLEM: LACK OF DIFFERENTIATION

Product differentiation creates layers of insulation because buyers have preferences and product loyalties, and there is a high level of product differentiation in the overall investment management market – based on financial performance, charges and levels of service. Within the private client sector the level of differentiation is much lower, for two main reasons.

First, the majority of the players in the market are offering the same services to the same client groupings. Level of service and charges do not differ significantly from bank to bank; investment performance is not likely to differ dramatically from institution to institution. Certainly the majority of the private banking institutions have a very similar approach to their stock selections and recommended asset allocations. It is broadly true to say that the investment mix for any given private client portfolio will be the same from fund manager to fund manager, although there will be differences in investment performance based on the nature and timing of stock selection and asset allocation.

Second, competitive differentiation is influenced by the level of client knowledge and experience. Those looking for a private bank or private client fund manager for the first time have only a very limited amount of information immediately available. There is almost nothing in the way of investment performance rankings or clear indications of the levels of service that will be provided. For any potential client wishing to appoint a private fund manager, the only effective means of determining the different merits of separate institutions is to meet directly with the account directors.

Established clients have a better understanding of the market and the level of service that they can expect to receive. However, unless they have a detailed knowledge of the service and investment performance achieved by other firms, generally only available through friends or relatives that may bank with a rival firm, there is little information on which to make an objective assessment. As a result, those clients that choose to switch advisors will do so generally out of a strong sense of dissatisfaction with the level of service and performance, rather than in the expectation of even better service elsewhere.

'GREED IS OUR ONLY COMPETITOR'[6]

The private client market is highly fragmented, with a wide choice of institutions facing the personal investor. The different competitors are taken to include not only the better known private banking institutions, but also regional stockbrokers, law firms and accountants.

The number of private banking institutions alone has shown substantial growth over the last decade, in response to the growth of personal wealth. In a number of cases investment management firms have expanded their small private client service in an effort to attract a range of new business, either by increasing the scope of funds which they are ready to manage, or by increasing their geographical coverage. In other cases, institutional asset managers have attempted to increase their range of financial products by offering private client services. The private client services are able to draw on the experience, research capabilities and dealing networks of the institutional business.

Table 2.21 Individual bank expense ratios, 1993

Bank	Expense ratio
Midland	70.4
NatWest	64.6
Barclays	64.1
Lloyds	61.5
Crédit Lyonnais	74.1
Banque National de Paris	72.8
CCF	71.4
Swiss Bank Corporation	66.6
UBS	65.3
Crédit Suisse	57.5
Deutschebank	72.1
Dresdner Bank	70.3
Commerzbank	67.4

Source: The Bankers Magazine, 1993

The league table of bank expense ratios, shown in Table 2.21, makes it very clear why larger banks are keen to expand their private banking operations: as off-balance-sheet activities, and with high potential for fee income, the ROCE (Return on Capital Employed) could contribute significantly to improved ratios.

The impact of the 1987 stock market crash severely hit investor confidence and much of 1988 and 1989 involved a rebuilding of confidence in both the institutional and private sectors. The decline in investor confidence hit the private banking sector hard when the volume of client dealings fell away, thereby hitting the level of commission income. The difficulties of Lloyds Names has also affected the UK market. As a result, the private banks have sought other forms of income, which have come from an extension of different products and services, including financial advice and planning.

COSTING THE COMPETITION

The nature of the private banking client means that costs (to the client) are of far less importance than in other banking sectors. Service and performance are the selection criteria. Problem areas for private bankers are higher cost pressures and lower client activity level: pressures in these two factors during the late 1980s and early 1990s brought minimum fund sizes down in some cases.

Fixed costs are high: information technology is a key requirement to supply the swiftest, most relevant range of information to portfolio managers, and enough power to produce complex analyses. Human resources will continue to be the major investment since, more than many other industry sectors, this is a people business.

Clients move their private banking business infrequently, and so the cost of switching plays a very small part in determining competitive market levels.

Competition may be more pronounced between domestic organisations and branch or regional offices of foreign institutions. The latter can often use their foreign nature as a loss leader. Professional advisors operating within a niche must act as a barrier between client and banker, but may in turn generate transaction business.

HINWI clients do have relatively high bargaining power, since they frequently are members of a family, professional or business grouping. Individual dissatisfaction can very quickly affect quite a large sector of business; standard customer service lore shows that a single client's dissatisfaction is likely to 'infect' a further nine clients, and at a minimum $1m level per client, it is not the sort of business any bank would like to lose. Servicing client demands or expectations may prove difficult, with little flexibility for adjustment to charges or swift development of new products.

OFFSHORE BANKING: A GROWTH AREA?

It is clear that a high proportion of investible assets of wealthy individuals are managed outside their domicile, i.e. 'offshore'. Chase argues that 60 per cent of total offshore wealth is destined for Europe, with the bulk of it going to Switzerland. Europe is in turn the source of 35 per cent.

A major impetus for private banking clients is having their funds protected from and out of the reach of fiscal authorities: it follows that 'offshore' is not so much a category as an essential requirement of the increasing client numbers.

Table 2.22 Fund flows for private banking

Source		Destination	
Europe	35%	Switzerland	35%
Middle East	15%	UK	15%
Latin America	15%	Channel	6%
Asia	15%	Islands	
Other	20%	Luxembourg	6%
		US	12%
		Caribbean	10%
		Hong Kong	5%
		Other	11%

Source: Chase Manhattan Private Bank, 1993

EMERGING MARKETS

While the emergence of new markets in the Asia Pacific and Latin American regions is attracting a lot of interest from corporate bankers, private bankers understand very well that a key component of wealth management is wealth preservation. Thus wealthy individuals prefer to minimise their risk, or at least to contain it to sums which they are prepared to set aside for greater risk-orientation, while maintaining their capital in separate investments. Certainly, although there is clear appreciation of the opportunities which may become apparent in Central and Eastern Europe, very few private bankers are prepared to advise their clients to invest there. (Indeed, Japanese and American investment banks appear to be pulling out of the corporate finance market in the area, as many of them close branches.)[7] At the same time, because of the requirement for due diligence, and knowledge of the beneficial owner of funds, bankers are extremely cautious in accepting new clients from those regions which appear unstable.

Most change is appearing where individuals have left their home countries and are now prepared to repatriate funds to support growth, for example in some countries of Latin America. In the past, there was a high flow of capital from the region to offshore centres; now capital is needed to strengthen their economies for future growth. Client needs there are not as clearly defined yet as they are in the Asian market: there are smaller stock exchanges, of lesser importance, and clients often prefer time deposits. Funds created as 'country' funds, however, are benefiting from above average returns, and are particularly successful in Switzerland, where Swiss franc (SFr) investors see real opportunity for diversity. Indeed, it seems that Latin America is experiencing a deluge of foreign money: in 1992 a total of $60 billion flowed into the region, with private flows to the region doubling to $35 billion.

It remains to be seen whether these capital flows will be sustained over the long term, as they have been in Asia, which as a whole benefited little from the growth of private flows in 1992 – up only $1 billion over 1991. However, with $40 billion in 1992, Asia still receives the largest share of private flows. The major expansion of private flows in Asia took place between 1989 and 1990, when they more than doubled to $38 billion; Latin America's big jump occurred in 1992. Only a relatively small number of countries accounted for the bulk of the growth in private flows in 1992 – in Asia, the United Arab Emirates and China, India and Indonesia; in Latin America, Mexico, Brazil, Argentina and Venezuela. The distribution of these flows is more dependent on risk and return considerations than other financial flows, and the countries which have been able to attract private flows broadly share the following common features:

- their growth performance has been good, and significantly higher than that recorded in the OECD area;
- they have maintained or restored macroeconomic stability through the last decade (i.e. control over inflation, fiscal consolidation, exchange rate stability);
- they have undertaken major structural reforms in areas such as trade and foreign direct investment liberalisation, deregulation and deepening of the domestic financial system, capital account opening, and downsizing the role of the state in economic activity;
- they have avoided major disruptions with the international financial community, or succeeded in putting their debt service obligations back on a more sustainable basis.

By comparison, the performance of the vast majority of the other developing countries has been poorer, and their commitment to reform less evident. In addition, they have been hampered by a number of other factors – limited local or regional markets, underdeveloped banking and financial systems, discretionary approaches to allocation, poor labour quality and infrastructure, depressed markets for raw materials and agricultural products, and political uncertainty – all of which have contributed to their unattractiveness to private finance.

Table 2.23 indicates the increased private capital flow into emerging market regions.

Table 2.23 Total net resource flows from OECD countries to developing countries: constant $ billion

Private flows	1984	1985	1986	1987	1988	1989	1990	1991	1992
Direct investment *of which*:	19.7	11.3	15.2	24.0	25.0	30.7	27.9	26.4	28.8
Offshore centres	6.7	6.4	8.1	13.3	10.2	7.5	7.3	6.5	6.3
International bank	30.3	26.3	9.8	8.6	8.9	12.1	15.5	11.0	37.7
lending *of which*:	−10.6	20.8	−5.6	6.1	4.6	9.2	7.3	12.0	23.6
Total bond lending	0.0	7.3	1.4	−0.1	1.7	1.5	4.7	13.0	13.4
Other private	0.5	2.3	1.8	1.3	4.8	3.1	5.3	6.6	9.0
Grants by NGOs	4.6	5.0	4.6	4.9	4.8	4.6	5.3	5.2	5.2

Source: OECD *Financial Market Trends*, October 1993

Table 2.24 Liquid assets investment requirements

Bank	Bias	Minimum investment value	Other segmentation
ANZ-Grindlays	UK	£50k	Discretionary: £250k
Bank Sarasin & Cie		£250k–500k	Average fund investment of £70k
Barclays Private Bank	UK International	£250k	
Chase Manhattan	International/ offshore	$1m	'52% of our client assets represent relationships with over $10m'
Citibank	International	$1m	
Coutts & Co.	UK International	£50k $1m	
Crédit Suisse		Not available	Segmented via holdings in variety of banking arms
Hardy & Co. Privatbankiers		Not available	Likely to be DM1m plus
J. P. Morgan		$2m	
Julius Baer & Cie			Can be £250k in London
Kleinwort Benson		£200k	Unit and investment trusts available for lower than £200k
Kredietbank			LFr20m – personal; advisory higher; portfolio management highest
Lombard, Odier & Cie		None	
Pictet & Cie		None	Typical client has SFr1m plus
Samuel Montagu/ HSBC		Not available	'$5m on deposit is an interesting client'
Swiss Bank Corporation		$1m	
Trinkhaus & Burkhardt/HSBC		DM1m	
Union Bank of Switzerland	UK	$1m	No upscale personal banking – 'leave that to the clearers'

Source: Business Interventions, 1993

NOTES

1 'Offshore' in this context is outside the individual's home country.
2 *Source*: Chase Manhattan estimates, based on US government statistics and Lorenz curve predictions, 1991.
3 Mintel.
4 *Source*: Utz Pfannschmidt's conference paper, 'Recreating independence for the private banker', IBC conference 'Success in private banking', London, March 1993. Herr Pfannschmidt is Managing Director of Hardy & Co. Privatbankiers.
5 *The Economist*, 26 February 1994.
6 Ivan Pictet, interview with the author, December 1993.
7 *Financial Times* report, 6 January 1993.

3

GETTING, KEEPING AND SERVING CLIENTS

THE CLIENT VIEWPOINT: DRIVING CHOICE

Understanding, and then managing, client expectation is the greatest problem for the private banker. As has already been seen, today's client has greater knowledge and sophistication – which means that there is also a far greater expectation of service and performance.

The importance of performance should not be underestimated. Many clients now are concerned with absolute, not relative performance: no matter that they have achieved a 2 per cent improvement on comparative indices; in recessionary and low interest rate times, what counts is the amount returned. In periods of high inflation, the argument for relative performance is easy to make: positive absolute performance can be associated with a positive decline in real wealth.

It is more imperative than ever for relationship officers to know their clients well, and to know their requirements even better. Techniques of benchmarking expected performance are of increasing value, as are a variety of measures of performance. Clients need some solid comparisons because, after all, they are investing their own money.

A great debate in private banking exists over product-orientation and client need. While it is clear that all banks rely heavily on a perception of service as a main attractor, there is no doubt that clients are sometimes attracted by a specific product, or package. This is particularly true of competitive bidding for client business.

Quite naturally, clients want to outperform markets when they are going up, and not to lose money when they are going down – an idealised desire which is unfortunately not achievable. This means that management of clients' expectations must exclude underselling the possibilities, and overselling expected gains. Since expectations are largely determined by historic experience, when markets become more expensive and therefore more liable to produce poor results, the client is likely to be looking for mounting future returns. The hapless advisor may well be just as optimistic, and perhaps in the difficult position of wanting to develop short-term business in what should be a long-term relationship.

27

Certainly private banking satisfaction relies on brilliant service, and it is achievement against the myth of service which will differentiate between competitors. Customers are forgiving over many things, even over less than expected portfolio performance – but send out an incorrect statement, or forward mail to the wrong address, and considerable wrath will ensue.

Matching culture, skill and style between client and relationship officer is extremely important; not surprisingly, so is the bank's organisation. It is apparent that if the bank is not organised in a way which both appeals to, and supports the needs of, the client, the account is likely to be moved. There is little point in matching an investment expert with a client looking for a high value mortgage, for example. Similarly if the relationship is a good one, the clients may follow a change of employer for the account officer.

WHAT DO CLIENTS NEED?

It is generally agreed that clients of private banks primarily require something that helps them sleep at night – security for their money. In times of turbulence, with economic pressures and ethnic strife, wealth that has been carefully built up may well be at risk – from capital decrease if not from the pressures of conflict or crime.

Chase Manhattan's research showed that investors vary in their financial goals, but that 67 per cent choose a 'solid reputation' as the key characteristic of their private banker, and 57 per cent require a stable environment for their assets. The confidence and trust developed between client and relationship manager is key. The requirement to increase wealth substantially, though collecting 30 per cent in the rating, comes lower than the preservation of wealth and family protection against premature death.

Table 3.1 Investment objectives

Characteristic as one of top three goals	%
Finding a stable environment for assets	57
Preserving wealth against inflation and depreciation	55
Protecting family in case of premature death	45
Increasing wealth substantially	30

Source: Chase Manhattan Private Bank, 1993

Chase points out that their research shows a different profile according to geography: European clients value the personal relationship with their banker, including such factors as competence and continuity of service. They place slightly less emphasis on investment performance than on the need for their private bank to be old and established, unlike their counterparts in Asia who have a slightly greater risk appetite.

ABN-Amro, who have established a considerable presence in the Asia Pacific region, find that their clients have a somewhat different set of requirements. Safety is a characteristic required by only 30 per cent, whereas 50 per cent require a wide product range, and an unsurprising 90 per cent rank service as the key characteristic.

Table 3.2 Market needs

Characteristic ranked 1 or 2	%
Service	90
Wide product range	50
Safety	30
Investment performance	20
Convenience	10

Source: ABN-Amro Bank, 1994

Undoubtedly the extent of an individual's wealth will influence requirements: from the simple time deposit to the highly tailored portfolio of cash, securities, real estate and art. Also important is the development stage of the wealth lifecycle. When at the beginning of the lifecycle, transaction-oriented services are likely to be required: this may include a fund management bias, or a cash and equities portfolio. Income generation and preservation of liquidity will require money movement, trade execution (all markets) and cash flow management.

Movement into a phase of heavy commitment – perhaps marriage, a family, bigger or better property investment – is likely to bring a greater requirement for preservation of wealth against inflation and depreciation (the second highest category in Chase Manhattan's research). Careful attention to balancing client requirements is particularly necessary at this stage. Career progression, or perhaps entrepreneurial activity in founding or buying a business, and an associated increase in income, is likely to bring a greater expectation of wealth enhancement. There is a need to build equity, by financing purchases and investments, participation in major investment markets, and the purchase and liquidation of assets. And as careers reach their peak and retirement looms, retirement provision becomes paramount, along with concerns about distribution of wealth for descendants. Then comes asset protection and preservation: the minimising of levels of financial risk; insurance of life, health, and property. The provision of funds for retirement and estate management are enjoying an increase in Europe as the post-war generation of business builders disposes of assets.

Inherited wealth, of course, can produce entry to the wealth management lifecycle at any stage. Getting wealth management advice requires information regarding the status of all accounts and services, and the provision of dynamic information and analytics – share price movements, for example. This will of course include all the elements of identification of risk and opportunity in markets, planning assistance, and investment and financial advice.

A 1980s analysis of client needs established seven critical features of service delivery to the private client:

- Recognition: the provision and demonstration of client knowledge; consistent anticipation and meeting of needs.
- Confidentiality: limited access to financial and personal information, organised as the client wishes.
- Relationship continuity: maintenance of a predictable, intelligent, personalised partnership with the service provider.
- Expertise: provision of specialised and timely intelligence to the client to support decision-making.
- Choice: global access to products and information, with customisation as required.
- Financial control: guaranteed management of assets within a set framework.
- Safety and security: identification and minimisation of personal and financial risks.

Consistency is crucial: private banking service provision can be likened to McDonald's in its emphasis on fast customer response, highly professional client-facing personnel and a lack of problem presentation. Service individuality can only come from client knowledge.

CLIENT TURNOVER

Understandably any private banker worth their salt strives not to lose a valuable client. Inevitably, though, some clients move on: through dislike of the individual with whom they do business; dissatisfaction with performance; or from competitive measures by other players.

In tandem with their increased financial sophistication, clients have learnt that they can get more from a bank by splitting their wealth management across a number of institutions. With the increasing number and variety of client services available, it really is a buyer's market.

THE SPECIAL CASE: US CLIENTS AND EUROPEAN BANKS

Private banks abound in the US, with its tradition of the creation of entrepreneurial wealth. In this rather different context, private banks have supported their clients by providing them with credit services: high value mortgages are the biggest current offering and need, according to US Trust's Private Banking Division, which has a loan portfolio of $725 million, deposits of $635 million and $8.5 billion of client assets under management.

The implications for the European private bank expanding its operation in North America, or perhaps serving American expatriate clients, are clear: the provision of credit is established as an expected service. This presents the typical private bank in Europe with some difficulties. What lending exists is usually done on a Lombard credit basis (i.e. fully secured against the client's own portfolio); while private banks which are part of a global or retail operation may have skills in this area, it is not necessarily the case for smaller or more specialised players. Even so, Chase Manhattan Private Bank will not provide credit services to clients outside the US because of the difficulties of credit checking – unlike the infrastructure in their home country.

US Trust surveyed the top 1 per cent of wealthy individuals in America in 1993, and found that an overwhelming 93 per cent of those surveyed associated their financial success with a willingness to work hard, rather than being born into privilege. A large number of Americans consider a family-owned business as an extremely important source of wealth – some 46 per cent – while 33 per cent accumulated their wealth through corporate employment. Only 10 per cent cited inheritance as their source of wealth, although this is likely to change over the next generation.

It seems that affluent Americans have been living the 'American dream', with almost three-quarters of them describing their childhood economic situation as poor, or lower or middle class. Today, more than two-thirds (68 per cent) consider themselves at least upper middle class, while only 19 per cent consider themselves wealthy. This probably reflects the tendency for entrepreneurs to have their net worth tied up in the ownership of a business.

Table 3.3 Change in financial situation

Class perception	Self-described situation at 10 year of age	Self-described situation at present
Poor	9%	zero
Lower class	13%	1%
Middle class	48%	13%
Upper middle class	26%	68%
Wealthy	4%	19%

Source: US Trust survey, 1993

Chief worries among affluent Americans are the economy and long-term US prosperity. This naturally reflects concern regarding the financial well-being of their children and grandchildren, with around three-quarters of those surveyed subscribing to the view that it will be harder for the next generation to accumulate wealth. Clearly private bankers are in a strong position to offer trust and estate management services to assuage these fears.

The younger Americans surveyed had a number of different concerns: the potential insolvency of social security, the financial instability of institutions which manage and hold their investments, the inability financially to withstand a protracted period of illness, and the inability to save enough money to ensure a comfortable retirement. Significantly, they are worried that they will be providing financial support to their parents in addition to their children as they are saving for their own retirement.

Changing tax laws are another concern, which may have an impact on savings and investment behaviour. Affluent Americans currently save or invest 27 per cent of their after-tax income, a significant figure when compared to the 5 per cent savings rate of the average US citizen.

Table 3.4 Distribution of after-tax income

Savings and investment	27%
Housing utilities and maintenance	23%
Food and clothing	16%
Vacations and travel	12%
Children's expenses	8%
Charitable contributions	8%
Healthcare and insurance	6%

Source: US Trust survey, 1993

In general, wealthy American individuals regard themselves as 'risk-averse' – which has to be a plus point for the old-established private banks of Europe, particularly those of Switzerland. US Trust's figures suggest that 43 per cent consider themselves less willing to take risk in their investment portfolio than others; however, they none the less invest in opportunities which might be considered by others to be risky. Around two-thirds indicated that their financial investments had been an important factor in their wealth accumulation, and the spread of their portfolios shows a fine awareness of diversification and its benefits. The majority are more interested in long-term capital gains than in current yield, with intentions to allocate higher percentages of their portfolios to tax-exempt municipal bonds, private businesses and international stocks. They also plan to decrease their exposure to US government securities, gold, collectibles, cash equivalents, taxable corporate bonds, blue-chip stocks and real estate for investment purposes.

Table 3.5 Typical affluent portfolio

Real estate, future, options, partnerships, misc.	32%
Stocks/stock funds	29%
Bonds/bond funds	21%
Cash accounts	18%

Source: US Trust survey, 1993

Less than half of the wealthy individuals surveyed have used a financial planner, insurance agent, banker, retirement plan advisor or an asset manager to address the financial concerns expressed.

CLIENT ACQUISITION: THE BANKER'S VIEWPOINT

Client acquisition is perhaps one of the most mystical areas of private banking. With high levels of referral producing new clients, it would seem that the only requirement is a good image, some skilful public relations work and a happy client. But this approach has its problems, especially in the more competitive environment in which 1990s private bankers have to operate.

Sitting back and waiting for client referral is an extremely passive approach, and is not one, perhaps, to attract the more sophisticated client. Yet it certainly is the case that the old Pareto rule[1] continues to apply: 20 per cent of clients provide 80 per cent of assets under management. It is already clear, though, that a number of the bigger banks see increases in their market share as decreases in the share of their competitors; in other words, they all seem to be going after the same clients, for at least a proportion of their portfolio management, while largely ignoring the huge potential that appears to exist. Chase Manhattan, for example, forecasts no real growth in Europe other than by acquiring their competitors' clients, which clearly contrasts with their views on clients requiring European portfolio management, but who are non-European.

It appears, then, that customer acquisition, far from being a passive, referral-based activity, must be a focus area for banks determined to stay in the market. Of course there is no doubt that referral is the best method of gaining new or increased business: it implies that the referring customer is happy with the service with which he is being provided, and has a high regard for his banker.

However, banks are now starting to target areas, profiles and business requirements as a means of increasing their client base. The increasing competition in what was a rarefied market will demand greater and greater client acquisition skills.

ACTIVE SELLING OF PRIVATE BANKING SERVICES

Hands may be raised in horror at the thought of a relationship manager daring to ask for client introduction, or attempting to see the circle of friends and family. However, there is no doubt that some banks are becoming more assertive in their techniques, and are encouraging their relationship officers to be more active in their selling, as well as their marketing activities. Some clients, because of their requirement for confidentiality (if not secrecy) would not dream of letting their banker near a friend, colleague or family member.

For Swiss private banks, this is a move away from tradition: their image of only ever responding to client requests, or staying behind their desk until summoned, has had to change. US banks are showing the way in this field, as in so many others. Chase Manhattan, for example, classifies its private bankers in three ways: hunters, who develop new business; miners, who develop the existing client base; and servicers, who maintain the existing client base. The 'hunters' are 'super sales folk', difficult to keep and ideally selling for 100 per cent of their time: finding a new customer, bringing them in and going for another. (This does present some problems in the UK, given the FIMBRA rules on cold calling.) 'Miners' do the lion's share of business and provide significant growth, by their work in developing business with existing clients. Ensuring consistent good service is the role of the 'servicers', who probably deal with client administration rather than analysis.

Undoubtedly many clients do have an allegiance to banks which have served them well, providing a stability of base clients. But, as one Swiss banker pointed out, moving staff from a passive client acquisition stance to an active one can produce considerable benefit; getting to pro-active is a bonus.

THE COST OF ACQUISITION

Client acquisition is not a cheap process. A conservative estimate suggests that the first year of the relationship will be 'revenue-neutral'. This certainly does not take into account the fully loaded expense of running a relationship manager, or of the overhead expense to be assigned – fee income of 1.5 per cent on a $1m portfolio produces only $15,000, hardly enough to pay for a few foreign trips and the establishment of a high quality image. But when a client relationship has been established, and requires perhaps a couple of meetings and 50 phone calls in a year, it does indeed become profitable. With an ideal ratio of 1:50 clients – and in practice considerably more – the revenue generation can rapidly be increased. A well-known American bank is happy to gain 8–10 clients per month; Pictet

(London) has a target of 10 per cent plus, while Barclays International Private Bank feels that a 15 per cent annual growth in client assets under management can readily be bettered.

Business introducers are not so common as may be imagined, yet are a potential source of cost-effective acquisition. Accountants, for example, are being actively courted by some UK banks, both as a source of interest themselves and as sources of referral. Attempts to differentiate between existing client referral, internal staff referral and referral from business-to-business relationships are not fruitful: whether banks are able to differentiate or whether they prefer not to say is debatable! An educated guess, though, is that business introduction referral is less than 10 per cent; internal leveraged referral generates 30–40 per cent, and client referral 50–60 per cent. The success or failure of any kind of reference of course depends on a *quid pro quo* for the introducer, which is an area for attraction. Citibank, for example, makes a point of treating their own visiting relationship managers as private clients themselves, in the secure knowledge that they will then happily recommend clients who require services outside their home geography.

CLIENT RETENTION

Hanging on to a client is important for every business, and crucial for the private bank. It is well known that while the loss of one customer may not be important in the numbers game, the nine people he tells of his dissatisfaction, and the likely snowball effect, are. According to research by the Royal Bank of Scotland, it is five times cheaper to retain a client than to gain a new one. Analysis of the value of acquisition channels by the American VIP Forum shows that the break-even point does not occur until year four of the client–bank relationship, even though there may be revenue over the whole of the initial five years.

The Royal Bank of Scotland uses a complex relationship marketing system to evaluate client acquisition costs and profitability; acquisition costs cover promotional, processing and response rate operations, but the greatest initial cost is in customer intelligence. Prioritisation of actual and latent profitability provides the bank with an effective communication strategy, based on knowledge of client attitudes and the resulting ability to manage client expectations.

Profitability analysis is a crucial element of client retention, since it identifies the customers which a bank cannot afford to lose. Indeed, such an analysis of Citibank's international private customer base resulted in the development of its separately constituted private banking business. By analysing client profitability, it is possible to identify the services that the most profitable clients need, thus supporting a market-led service; to make sure that they are satisfied, and not gained by competitors; and to establish the break-even cost of services for 'the rest', which can be used to fix the costing and pricing levels for the bank overall.

RELATIONSHIP OFFICERS

As the pivotal person holding the attraction between client and bank, the relationship officer's skill is crucial. Although knowledge of financial instruments and portfolio management is a clear need, other facets assume as great if not greater importance. Of course, good interpersonal skills are essential: the ability to build up rapport and establish trust. The difficult grey area of identification with client or bank means that any relationship officer must have a depth of assertiveness: the ability to serve the client without being bullied into untenable positions. Language skills help – indeed, are necessary – in this international environment.

A fairly recent change in private banking structural approaches to relationship management is to separate out portfolio management responsibility. Recognition of the need for specialist knowledge in a complex world, and of the pure customer-oriented time demands, have led many organisations to create high quality teams in support of client groups. Thus the relationship manager will have overall responsibility for client satisfaction, and a full understanding and monitoring of needs against service delivery. Supporting him (and they are mostly male) will be a portfolio manager, charged with achieving the best possible return, and further specialists who can construct or advise on complex/financial instruments, e.g. derivatives.

Success criteria for relationship managers vary from bank to bank, and may be team-oriented rather than purely individual. Typical expectations are gains in client business, high quality of business (for which read good fee income) and minimal loss of business. Other sectors of the banking community could learn much from the very clear and necessary focus on client service before all else. In J. P. Morgan's view, the bank has been more successful than others because they have kept the focus on the fact that the client comes first, and have got everybody into that way of thinking.[2] For Crédit Suisse, the emphasis is not just on profitability of the assigned portfolios, but on increase of assets (which implies client loyalty), and the team behaviour of the account officer. For the more traditional private Swiss bank, the portfolio and relationship managers are not regarded as profit centres but are assessed on a very individual basis. Pictet & Cie, for example, take into account the difference between high client esteem and new business creation, and asset management performance, and emphasise what is given to the bank, the 'spirit' in which an individual works.

All of the banks also recognise the need for an extra dimension to the rapport established between client and bankers, that of appropriate skill. Coutts & Co. in the UK, for example, take care to match an experienced and learned lender to a client requiring fund-raising activity, and an investment manager with buyers of investment products. Chase Manhattan emphasises the need for a variety of nationalities in their European business: all staff in the European operation are of European origin (currently some 12 nationalities), providing a good appreciation of cultural requirements as well as language skills.

The number of clients a relationship officer has depends on the mix of business and can vary between 50 and 500. In Switzerland, a typical level of responsibility is for SFr400–500m in client assets, generating annual revenue of SFr1m. However, significantly higher net worth clients, with in excess of $10 million, are managed on the ratio of 1:10. Relationship managers and their teams must understand the profitability of their products, but must equally balance this business imperative against a business ethos that decries a commission-focused approach to the job.

STAFFING: THE KEY TO RETAINING CLIENTS

Certainly the UK market saw an increase in search and recruitment for private banking staff during the last quarter of 1993 – undoubtedly linked to the recognition of new opportunities with the growing market and an increase in competitive organisations. Senior bankers are disturbed as much by potential staff turnover as they are by client turnover; the whole premise of private banking is based on longevity. The movement of an entire team from Lloyds Private Bank to Merrill Lynch, for example, is an indication of increasing growth and competition; private bankers in the Asia Pacific rim are poached with regularity.

No loss of client is acceptable, but some of the more aggressive banks do see a turnover rate of between one and two per month. Again, this may be segmented. Middle Eastern clients, for example, have not been slow in hiring ex-bankers as their own professional advisors and financial managers: people who are not required to maintain loyalty or allegiance. Growth in this trend may provide yet another facet of banking disintermediation, this time in its most profitable sector.

Investment in training for all private banks is an increasing requirement: clearly in knowledge of economics, financial markets, instruments, portfolio analysis and so on. Behavioural and management skills are as important, and are receiving greater focus, along with an emphasis on team building and working. A problem for Anglo-Saxon organisations has been the need to regard the 'bottom line' as bible, which has encouraged individual and short-term profit-orientation at the expense of communication and collaborative working methods.

Recognition of this as a potential problem has been translated by Chase into a range of compensation practices to promote the desired staff behaviour. Some banks still expect part of the value of a sale to be split with other technical experts on a client call – a practice almost guaranteed to delay the use of expertise until absolutely necessary, and thus detrimental to the client's requirements.

DOING THE WEEDING

As important as retaining a client, for some of the larger banks at least, is the weeding out of those whose assets or activity do not match up to expectations. If a client is going through hard times – perhaps suffering as a Lloyds Name, for example – the bank is likely to be sympathetic and look for future gains; if there is an inclination to keep an account going simply for holiday trips and utility bills, an investigation of potential is likely and the client may well be advised that 'another bank may be able to meet your needs more appropriately'. Pressure from senior management to ensure levels of activity are common in the Anglo-Saxon banking world, and pervade private banking too. Reasons for encouragement to move include a loss of net worth; a lack of business; and a loss of quality of investment.

In February 1992, Sir Dennis Weatherstone, Chairman and CEO of J. P. Morgan, said:

> We discourage potential clients who only have need of a more traditional cheque cashing/money transfer service. We tell them that there are other institutions better able to take care of that at more reasonable prices. If they were to bank with us, they would find the charges were more appropriate to someone who needed the kind of services that we supply in the investment area and it would be uneconomic for them to use our services.

NOTES

1 Pareto was an Italian mathematician who analysed the physical movements of stocks in component warehouses a century ago; his theorem is that the minority of any activity produces the bulk of the desired result. Thus, 20 per cent of clients produce 80 per cent of the profits.
2 *Banking World* interview with Sir Dennis Weatherstone, Chairman and CEO of J. P. Morgan, February 1992.

4

EUROPEAN PROFILES I

THE SWISS EFFECT

No review of private banking activity can possibly overlook Switzerland. With a history of an absence of war since the sixteenth century, Switzerland has maintained its aura of stability and safety for a considerable period. Government continues to be stable, and there is very little social unrest; only five years ago the prospect of unemployment in Switzerland was extremely remote, and crime figures low. Thus one of the primary requirements of the private banking client – stability – is very well served by the Swiss.

THE BANKING SECTOR'S OVERALL CONTRIBUTION TO THE SWISS ECONOMY

The banking sector employs 3.5 per cent of the country's working population, who generate more than 8 per cent of GDP (1991 figures). In 1992, direct taxes paid by Swiss banks and finance companies in Switzerland and abroad amounted to SFr1.6bn. Some 93 per cent of the activity of Swiss banks is carried out in Switzerland, which implies that the banking sector is an important source of tax to the country. Research by Chase Manhattan estimates that around one-third of the world's $2.1 trillion offshore funds are invested with banks in Switzerland.

At the end of 1991 the balance sheets of Switzerland's banks and finance houses totalled SFr1.115bn, over four times the country's national income. By comparison, US banks' balance sheets amount to about half the US national income. According to Andersen Consulting's report on *Swiss Banks to the Year 2000*, the cleaning-up operation of the Swiss financial market initiated at the end of the 1980s will continue: with global entanglement of the finance markets, and an overall trend towards deregulation, the Swiss banks are strengthening their international alliances. They are also sharpening management skills and developing innovation, improving productivity and, of course, rationalising to counteract margin erosion and loss of profitability.

From 1981 to 1991, the average annual growth rate of value added of the banking sector was about 4 per cent. In comparison, growth rate of GDP was only 1 per cent over the same period.

Table 4.1 Bank system in Switzerland, 1992: comparative sizes

Bank group	Portion of aggregate assets of the banks	Number of institutes
Cantonal banks	20.8	28
Major banks	49.4	4
Regional and savings banks	7.8	174
Credit and 'Raffeisen' banks	3.4	2*
Other Swiss banks (1)	7.2	93
Finance companies	1.7	101
Foreign banks (2)	9.2	148
Private bankers	0.5	19
Total bank system	100.0	569

Source: Swiss National Bank
Notes:
(1) Other banks excluding foreign-controlled banks
(2) Foreign-controlled banks and branches of foreign banks
* Two associations with almost 1,200 member banks.

The Basle Committee for Bank Supervision within the Bank for International Settlement (BIS) issued recommendations for harmonising capital adequacy regulations in 1989. Such regulations impose restrictions on the amount of lending in relationship to a bank's capital, and capital adequacy requirements continue to be strictest in Switzerland. In competitive terms, Swiss banks operate at a disadvantage to foreign banks, in using their own capital to a greater extent. Overall requirement is for 6.35 per cent, against 6.02 per cent for the US, 2.46 per cent in Japan and 3.59 per cent in Germany. The Swiss requirement is broken down to provide adequacy ratios of 2 per cent for bills of exchange and money market paper; 2 per cent for securities; 2 per cent for current account credits; and between 4 and 6 per cent for claims on banks.

At the end of 1992 there were 569 banks and finance companies operating in Switzerland. Of the 460 banks, 320 were Swiss-controlled. Foreign assets make up around 35 per cent of the aggregate balance sheet total of Switzerland's banks, a figure which rises to over 50 per cent if trust funds are included, higher than for banks in the US, Japan or Germany.

Swiss banking is clearly a leading export industry for the country. Roughly every third Swiss franc earned by banks comes from services to foreigners or capital invested abroad. Banks' net exports are slightly higher than those of the chemical industry, outrank tourism and dwarf machinery.

SWISS PRIVATE BANKING IN THE LAST 100 YEARS

For centuries, Basle and Geneva were Switzerland's main financial centres. Zurich's rising importance in the financial sector began with the construction of the railway, the development of the machine-tool industry and the founding of the modern Swiss state in 1848. Later, with the construction of the airport, and a new concentration of banks and television, Zurich also became a leading financial centre in Switzerland.

During the twentieth century, the Swiss banks earned their reputation for stability and secrecy. The neutrality established by the Congress of Vienna in 1815 was carefully guarded during the Second World War; the famous (or infamous) numbered account was introduced to conceal German flight capital from the Nazis. The Banking Law of 1934 confirmed the principles of secrecy, which precluded the US government from confiscating German assets held in Swiss accounts for war reparations.

After the war, with a strong franc, Switzerland found itself becoming a major capital exporter, by value of its attractiveness to investors. A former partner of Lombard, Odier put it thus: 'Having been a country of refuge we were also a country of international fund management.'

During the 1960s, substantial foreign private funds began to flow in: first from the US, and then as a result of political unrest in Europe, Latin America and the Middle East. The Iraqi invasion of Kuwait in 1990 sparked a massive inflow of flight capital again; some estimates suggest that in just three months, more money came in than at any other time in the country's history. In the late 1980s, the Far East boom created a new and fertile ground for new clients.

SECTOR GROWTH

Swiss private banks are extremely reluctant to disclose statistics on their assets. However, it has been claimed that asset management grew at 10 per cent (compound) during the 1980s. Client asset growth is said to be at 15 per cent a year. Traditional private banks do not take in savings deposits from the public, and do not have to publish their balance sheets. Interestingly, this also prevents Swiss banks from publicly promoting their services in Switzerland: their marketing focuses on product, rather than the actual bank. Asset management and fiduciary transactions are in any case off-balance-sheet, and it appears that the private banks' portion in the aggregate assets of the bank sector is a modest 0.5 per cent, or SFr5.9bn (1992 figures). However, funds managed are estimated at 7 per cent of total funds administered by all Swiss banks.

THREATS TO THE BANKING SECTOR IN SWITZERLAND

Political and economic advantages offered by Switzerland are no longer exclusive. Political stability can be offered by other states, and other countries also have strong currencies. In addition, the integration of European markets is progressing, with other financial centres improving their competitive position as a result of improved social and political environments. Following the general globalisation and internationalisation of the financial centres, the Swiss banking sector sees itself as more exposed to influence from outside the country and to greater international competition.

Table 4.2 Market participation change foreseen in next five years

	Decrease ⩾25%	10–25%	Up to 10%	No change	Increase
Independent property managers	2.5	15.5	38	16	28
Foreign banks	3	16	34	23	24
Financial institutions	2.5	15.5	30	35	17
Brokers	6	19	38	28	9
Private banks	2	15	58	23	2

Source: Andersen Consulting, 1992

Andersen's survey results, shown above, indicate a 24 per cent expectation that the presence of foreign banks will increase; against that, some 58 per cent of respondents expect the number of private banks to decrease by up to 10 per cent, and to a lesser degree, 15 per cent expect a decline of between 10 and 25 per cent.

Switzerland has started to introduce more flexible fee arrangements among the banks. With the elimination of securities transaction commission rate controls in 1991 by the Swiss Cartel Commission, private banking fees have become more competitive. Total fees now range typically between 0.8 per cent and 1 per cent of a client's assets under management.

Revisions to the Swiss stamp duty on securities transactions took effect in March 1993. The duty had previously been assessed on all securities transactions. The revision abolishes the duty on certain transactions, such as fixed income instruments by foreign investors.

THE CHALLENGES FOR SWISS PRIVATE BANKING

If the strict definition of private banker, rather than private banking is used, only 18 Swiss banks can lay claim to the name. However, the function of private banking, as has already been discussed, is one that attracts many players: the big banks, private banks, asset management banks and *gérants de fortune*. Members of the Association of Swiss Private Bankers operate their firms as partnerships, each partner having unlimited liability for the assets and liabilities of his company. Eighteen such banks exist in Switzerland.

Unfortunately the level of democracy in Switzerland can sometimes backfire, as was seen with the 1993 referendum on membership of the European Economic Area (EEA). When the people voted against membership, the politicians were left with egg on their faces. However, the impact on private banking in the country was certainly not negative: more funds flowed in as Switzerland apparently protected its status as a haven from disturbance, prying eyes and the reach of the tax man.

Table 4.3 Traditional Swiss private banks, 1993

Bank	Main location	Other locations	Established
Baumann & Cie	Basle		
Bordier & Cie	Basle		1844
Darier, Hentsch & Cie	Geneva	Lausanne, Zurich, Monaco, Nassau, Cayman, Montreal, Hong Kong, Tokyo	1796
Falck & Cie	Lucerne		1875
Goret & Cie	Geneva	Nassau	1845
E. Gutzmiller & Cie	Basle	Represented in Geneva, Zurich and Frankfurt	1886
Hentsch, Chollet & Cie	Lausanne	Association with Darier, Hentsch	1882
Hugo Kahn & Co.	Zurich		1923
Kottinger & Cie	Zurich/ Geneva	Affiliations in Paris and Luxembourg	1786
Landolt, Lonfat & Cie	Lausanne		
La Roche & Co.	Basle		1787
Lombard, Odier & Cie	Geneva	London, Amsterdam, Gibraltar, Montreal	1798
Mirabaud & Cie	Geneva	Montreal, Nassau, London, Taipei	1819
Pictet & Cie	Geneva	Zurich, London, Luxembourg, Hong Kong, Tokyo, Montreal, Nassau	1805
Rahn & Bodmer	Zurich		1750
Bank Sarasin & Cie	Basle	Zurich, London, Washington, Guernsey; represented in Hamburg and Mexico City	
Tardy, de Watteville & Cie	Geneva	Fribourg, Luxembourg	1904
Wegelin & Cie	St Gallen		1741

Source: Business Interventions, 1993

Geneva's Groupement des Banquiers Privées Genevois has as members the five banks who form the heart of the Swiss private banking ethos. The two biggest are Pictet, and Lombard, Odier, and both manage institutional as well as private client funds. Indeed, Pictet argue that private banking cannot continue to develop without the institutional side: the requirement for superb research and analysis and highly effective computer systems forms a tight link between the two sectors.

The number of traditional private banks has shrunk over the last 20 years: in 1976 there were 28, and by the end of 1993 only 18. One important problem is in sustaining the partnership basis: new partners of sufficient status and wealth are not abundant, and the cost base continues to rise. An estimate by consultants McKinsey & Co. indicates that a minimum critical mass of SFr7bn in assets under management is necessary for private bank survival, and Andersen Consulting made a similar point on the need for a strong capital base in their 1992 report. Different strategies have evolved: many private banks have been taken over by bigger banks; some maintain their independent operation as subsidiaries; Bank Julius Baer went public in 1981, as did Vontobel in 1986. In 1987, Basle-based Bank Sarasin sold some share capital; TDB-CBI Union Bancaire Privée was part-owned by American Express in an earlier flirtation with Swiss private banking.

Foreign banks in Switzerland see the location as a prime asset, and private banking as a product to offer on a global basis. Some have had less than superb experiences in Switzerland: Chemical Bank, State Street Bank & Trust Company and Security Pacific pulled out, and others have scaled back their operations. It seems to some that private banking in Switzerland does not depend on global services, but it does require presence or representation in the main financial centres. Yet others have made a success of their Swiss operation: Citibank, Chase Manhattan, Bankers Trust and Merrill Lynch, for example. UK banks Barclays and Coutts see Switzerland as a pivotal part of their private banking expansion.

The smaller operators in this world are the *gérants de fortune*. As small independent counsellors, frequently ex-bank employees, they act as middle men between bank and clients. Changes in brokerage commissions in 1991 have meant a move towards performance-based fees. Like the personal

Table 4.4 Bank groupings: share of total overall balance

	1960	1970	1985	1991
Major banks	29.7	45.0	50.7	48.6
Foreign banks	—	—	9.8	8.3
Financial institutions	1.5	2.7	2.5	1.9
Affiliated foreign banks	1.4	2.3	2.1	1.4
Private banks	2.4	1.1	0.5	0.5

Source: Swiss National Bank, 1992

advisors fully employed by HINWIs, particularly in the Middle East, this category presents a particular strand of competition for the banks. A further complication exists for the bank in not having a deepening relationship with the real client, but only with the advisor.

Rising costs and falling revenues, notwithstanding the outstanding results of 1993, have caused many Swiss banks to review their businesses. Technology is expensive; the high requirement for expertise in relationship management, portfolio management, specialists in investment techniques and supporting staff to keep track of legal and taxation matters means that private banking is a people-intensive business, another costly factor.

Active marketing seems to be a non-option in this very discreet business, though perhaps it is more useful to the fund managers; not all private banking clients are fabulously wealthy, and the smaller accounts, of around SFr1m, are not necessarily highly profitable. Cost of client acquisition is thought to be high, with selling cycles sometimes extending over two or three years, but in truth few banks can quantify the cost of client acquisition.

Switzerland's market share suffers from competitive erosion from other offshore centres. Luxembourg and the Channel Islands are the leading contenders; Singapore, the Cayman Islands, Gibraltar, Malta, Madeira, the Bahamas and the British Virgin Islands all figure in the fight to capture cash flows.

Structural changes, as in other countries, have produced rationalisation in the banks: more than 20 banks disappeared between 1991 and 1993 as a result of takeovers or mergers. These changes are largely outside the sphere of the private banks, but not entirely. The merge of Hentsch & Cie, founded in 1796, with Darier & Cie, established in 1837, produced Darier Hentsch & Cie in 1991; Crédit Suisse's parent company, CS Holding, bought Bank Leu in a hostile takeover bid in 1990, and owns Bank Hofman, Clariden Bank, Bank Heusser & Fundus Treuhand, as well as taking over Swiss Volksbank in 1993. In their November 1992 study, consultants Arthur Andersen predict that the number of banks operating in Switzerland is likely to decline by a hundred by the middle of the decade.

Table 4.5 Nominal changes in the balance sheets of bank groupings, 1987–91: percentage change on previous year

	1987	1988	1989	1990	1991
Major banks	5.5	4.9	5.4	2.7	3.8
Foreign banks	3.0	16.0	6.8	(7.5)	2.0
Financial institutions	2.4	11.3	10.6	(1.1)	(15.6)
Affiliated foreign banks	9.4	21.0	14.0	(32.6)	(17.7)
Private banks	18.9	(8.5)	11.9	(0.8)	(4.4)

Source: SNB statistics, 1992

Monetary problems are, of course, extremely complex, and a great deal of external influence of an extremely varied nature is exercised on the Swiss banks. Some of the key influencers are:

- The Swiss National Bank: as central bank, the SNB is the monetary authority of the Swiss state. It is independent of the government, cannot be financed by taxes, and has three functions: to follow a credit and monetary policy serving the overall interests of the country; to regulate the country's money circulation; and to facilitate payments traffic.
- The Federal Banking Commission: the FBC represents the supervisory authority of the banks, and safeguards depositor protection.
- Parliament, government and administration: at confederation level, banking is primarily within the Department of Finance; legislation and its application are of course its activity.
- The Cartel's Commission.
- The European Community.
- The European Free Trade Association (EFTA) is the association of European countries not holding EC membership.
- The European Economic Area (EEA): the creation of a common market for members of the EC and EFTA (except Switzerland) is a task within the EEA.
- BIS: the Bank of International Settlement.
- General Agreement on Tariffs and Trade (GATT).
- The European Bank of Reconstruction and Development (EBRD).

For the present, there is no question of Swiss membership in the European monetary system (EMS), as it would forestall the decision on possible membership in the European Economic Space (Community of EFTA and EC countries) or in the European Community. As a small, export-oriented country, Switzerland will need to integrate its monetary policy into Europe at some stage.

Swiss interest in efforts to set up a private market economy in the states of Central and Eastern Europe is considerable, and may produce new impetus for Swiss banks comparable with their financing of industrial expansion over the last two centuries. In addition the banks see an opportunity to provide knowledge, experience and knowhow, and have been active in setting up training programmes between banks and federal authorities. Switzerland participates as a member of the EBRD with a contribution of around SFr410m, and has a seat on the board of directors.

From a private banker's perspective, there are few legitimate clients emerging in the region, and those that are gain their fortune primarily from land sales. In a time of extensive change in the area, too, opportunities for criminal activity is similarly extensive, and thus Central and Eastern Europe is not an attractive client ground. Investment in the area is becoming more attractive, but largely through funds.

Table 4.6 Overseas share measured by balances, 1985–91

	Assets 1985	Assets 1991	Liabilities 1985	Liabilities 1991	SFr millions 1991
Major banks	52.0	49.2	40.7	44.3	543,187
Foreign banks	71.5	68.1	53.4	45.9	92,272
Financial institutions	87.8	79.9	65.2	55.7	20,929
Affiliated foreign banks	69.2	72.6	56.9	75.9	15,201
Private banks	32.0	25.7	37.7	26.9	5,334

Source: Swiss National Bank, 1992
Note: foreign activity of all banks except foreign affiliates decreased over the period. No individual trend is apparent for overseas liabilities share

Table 4.7 Switzerland's biggest fund managers:
a selection

Swiss-based funds	(SFr bn)
Union Bank of Switzerland	250–300
Crédit Suisse	230–280
Swiss Bank Corporation	200–250
Pictet & Cie	40
Lombard, Odier & Cie	30–35
Bank Julius Baer & Co.	30
Bank J. Vontobel & Co.	20–25
TDB-CBI Union Bancaire Privée	20–25
Darier, Hentsch & Cie	20
Citicorp Investment Bank	18–20
Banca della Suizzera Italiana	16–20
Bank Sarasin & Cie	15
Banque Paribas	5–10
Coutts & Co.	5–10
Guyerzeller Bank	5–10
Lloyds Bank	5–10
Societe Generale	5–10
Merrill Lynch	3–7

Source: B. Engstrom-Bondy and C. Makin, Swiss Banking in the 1990s, London, 1991

The Big Three universal banks and leading fund management banks all benefited considerably from the buoyancy and volatility of financial markets during 1993. Their income from market operations (gains made on securities and from ForeX trading) more than doubled in most cases. Strong growth in non-credit balance sheet business, coupled with the increase in the amount of funds under management, resulted in a sharp increase in commission fees. By contrast, virtually nil growth in balance sheet assets and an increase in the number of bad debt problems and arrears curbed the advance in net interest income.

Table 4.8 Interim figures for the Big Three universal banks, 1993: in SFr million

	Union Bank of Switzerland	%	As % of income	Swiss Bank Corp.	%	As % of income	Crédit Suisse Hold's	%	As % of income
Net interest income	5,480	+33	100	4,378	+34	100	6,499	+30	100
Net commissions	1,917	+11	35	1,508	+0	34	1,668	−1	26
Income from trading	1,932	+23	35	1,209	+20	28	2,233	+19	34
Total income	1,546	+144	28	1,554	+128	35	2,300	+74	35
Total charges	2,721	+15	50	2,202	+8	50	3,698	+21	57
Staff costs	1,933	+20	35	1,488	+16	34	2,638	+24	41
Overheads	788	+2	14	714	−5	16	1,060	+15	16
Total operating costs	2,759	+58	50	2,176	+75	50	2,801	+42	43
Gross pre-tax profits	1,074	+33	20	1,240	+66	28	1,336	+34	21
Group net profits	1,291	+87	24	719	+98	16	1,008	+61	16
Cash flow	2,365	+58	43	1,959	+77	45	2,344	+46	36

Source: Pictet & Cie
Note: these growth rates exclude the first time consolidation of Swiss Volksbank

Table 4.9 Interim figures for leading fund management banks, 1993: in SFr million

	Julius Baer	%	As % of income	BIL GT	%	As % of income	Leu Hold's	%	As % of income
Net interest income	299.3	+52	100	254.6	+25	100	352	+28	100
Net commissions	60.3	+11	20	63.5	+51	25	134	+17	38
Income from trading	113.1	+24	38	149.4	+16	59	123	+26	35
Total income	114.1	+168	38	41.7	+27	16	89	+89	25
Staff costs	159.1	+10	53	141.8	+10	56	182	+7	52
Overheads	103.2	+13	35	n/a	n/a	n/a	124	+2	35
Total operating costs	55.8	+4	19	n/a	n/a	n/a	58	+18	17
Gross pre-tax profits	140.2	+173	47	112.8	+50	44	170	+60	48
Deprec., prof., losses	42.7	+369	14	33.3	+60	13	50	+2	14
Group net profits	71.4	+117	24	69	+53	27	92	+124	26
Cash flow	114.1	+171	38	102.3	+55	40	142	+58	40

Source: Pictet & Cie

Table 4.10 Year-end results for universal and fund management banks, 1993:
in SFr million

	Swiss Bank Corp	% change	Crédit Suisse Hold's	% change	Julius Baer	% change	BIL-GT	% change
Net interest income	3,132	+1	3,232	+19	1,126.7	+15	128.1	+35
Income from holdings	66	−29	153	−18	—	—	—	—
Net commission income	2,575	+27	4,546	+40	250.4	+35	344.2	+36
Income from trading	2,905	+82	5,176	+123	237.4	+101	—	—
Sundry income	499	+142	706	+44	13.3	+6	81.0	+25
Total operating costs	4,701	+16	7,630	+40	343.6	+19	309.7	+20
Group net profits	1,403	+85	1,993	+69	146.9	+117	141.3	+74

Source: Pictet & Cie

In 1994, the picture was different – for UBS in particular. Group net profit fell by 28.9 per cent, and cash flow was down 24.6 per cent. Trading income was disappointing, although investment advisory and asset management services posted strong earnings. Fee and commission business remained the strongest source of revenues, posting a rise of 2.8 per cent to SFr4.157m. Investment advisory and asset management services made the biggest contribution of SFr3.204m to earnings in this sector, underlining the profitability and long-term potential of private banking services.

BANKING SECRECY

Banking secrecy is enshrined in Swiss law. The Swiss subscribe to the view that legal security, and the constitution's guarantee of protection for private property, depends for effectiveness on shielding individual financial circumstances from unauthorised view. Confidentiality is therefore provided by statutory protection, and was the catalyst for the creation of numbered accounts – accounts which could only be identified by a number, which was known to the client and a single bank manager only. This meant that other bank employees could not disclose information under pressure or coercion. Bank staff are legally obliged to observe bank secrecy, and can be prosecuted for infringement.

Over recent years, with the increase in potential for money laundering or transmission to apparently innocent accounts, a great deal of pressure has been put on the Swiss system for greater access – particularly by the US authorities. Bankers therefore exercise considerable caution when taking on new clients, with much attention to 'due diligence'. As a result of legislation introduced in 1990, banks may not accept any illegally acquired assets.

Banks are obliged to identify their customers as bona fide individuals, and if necessary to establish the identity of any beneficial owners other than the customer. In addition, the economic background and purpose of any transactions which appear unusual must be clarified. This includes querying the circumstances of an initial deposit of currency or precious metals to the value of over SFr25,000[1] at the beginning of a business relationship, and further deposits or withdrawals of significant amounts.

Given that private bankers expect a level of liquid assets well in excess of SFr 100,000 from their clients, the implications for an extremely careful developmental relationship are clear. 'Know your customer' is a maxim often repeated and refers to both understanding clients' needs, and the origin and legality of their transactions.

Banks of course impose controls to prevent illegal funds taking advantage of the banking system. The so-called banking 'supersecrecy' which allowed the beneficial owner of investments to use the services of a lawyer or notary has now also been abolished. As one private banker says, although there is a lot of hot money sloshing around the system, the trick is not to have any of it. Clients can, however, still hide their identities by using the vehicle of a trust or foundation in Liechtenstein. (See section on Liechtenstein, p. 51.)

CRIMINAL INVESTIGATIONS

If criminal activity is suspected or alleged, banks in Switzerland must furnish the prosecuting authorities with information requested, whether domestic or foreign. The authors of *Swiss Banking in the 1990s*[2] have this to say on Switzerland's position as a tax haven:

> World financial opinion says that Switzerland is a tax haven, sucking in funds that rightfully should be enriching other governments. Swiss bankers reply that their country is not a tax haven but a safe haven. . . . foreign funds parked in Swiss banks are 'not flight money, but fright money' as the Swiss insist.

Some estimates suggest, however, that up to half the total funds deposited in Switzerland are tax-sensitive. Even though cooperation is assured through the 1983 Swiss Law on International Legal Assistance, three categories of funds enjoy protection: those delivered from tax evasion, capital flight and the defiance of foreign exchange controls.

PENDING SWISS LEGISLATION

There are four significant projects concerning private banks in review by Swiss legal or government bodies.

1 Proposed amendments to the Federal Law on Banks and Savings Banks address the need for international consolidated banking supervision, among other subjects. Instances when foreign banks might supply information to head office in the interests of banking supervision would be

defined. The issue of whether the relevant foreign authorities may audit their Swiss branches and subsidiaries is under discussion.

2 The guidelines for the processing of international requests for information arising from legal action are being revised.

3 A bi-lateral treaty between Switzerland and the USA concerning various issues, including the fight against organised crime, is in revision.

4 An amendment to the Swiss penal code concerning the fight against money laundering has been in discussion for some time. At issue is a clarification as to whether banks will have the choice or the obligation to reveal a suspicious relationship to the legal authorities.

LIECHTENSTEIN

The principality of Liechtenstein, with its tiny area of only 62 square miles, boasts an advanced financial culture. As part of the Swiss financial centre, it shares Switzerland's secrecy arrangements, and of course has access to the country's capital markets and stock exchanges. Liechtenstein is a stable constitutional state, with a strong currency and no foreign exchange restrictions. It has good communications, extensive inward and outward investments, and a high cost of living. The capital is Vaduz, with a population of only 5,000; overall, the principality hosts a population of 28,500 of which 37 per cent are foreigners. German is the principal language. It is at the top of the European scale for *per capita* income, and there is very little unemployment.

The favourable tax climate makes Liechtenstein an important location for trusts and investment holdings, and for offshore sales companies. The degree of financial services demands a significant support sector of lawyers, tax advisors, accountants, etc.

Trusts and foundations of non-resident settlers are treated as taxable entities and taxed as domiciliary companies. In general, non-resident beneficiaries are exempt from Liechtenstein taxes; in 1989, trusts attracted annual capital tax of only 0.1 per cent on net assets.

Liechtenstein authorities played what might be seen as a clever hand as far as European union is concerned: unlike their Swiss neighbours, it was made clear to the population that joining the European Economic Space would be a good thing, whereas full membership of the EC might not. Membership of the EEA was thus duly approved by a referendum, and the principality has joined many of its other neighbours.

There are three main banks in Liechtenstein: BIL (Bank in Liechtenstein), VP Bank and Liechtenstein Landesbank; a new private bank, Neue Bank, was created in 1992. Neue Bank claims to work in the tradition of a classic private bank, with the share capital of employees generating a high identity with the bank. The bank offers property management, on the basis of full legal power, bonds, foreign exchange and precious metals trading, deposit and credit accounts, and of course, trust business. In 1990, Liechtenstein Landesbank's income from off-balance-sheet services comprised net commission income of SFr16.62m, an increase of 6.7 per cent. Total off-balance-sheet income covered 75 per cent of operating costs, and provided a net profit of SFr19.5m. Tremendous growth in the next two years brought a 47 per cent increase in profit to SFr29.0m in 1991, and a further 36.8 per cent to SFr39.7m in 1992.

Table 4.11 Selected results in SFr million: Liechtenstein private banks, 1992

	Neue Bank	VP Bank	BIL	Liechtenstein Landesbank
Commission income (net)	0.227	26.549	54.9	29.83
Sight deposits	16.258	443.07	265.35	292.58
Time deposits	91.408	2,640.42	3,932.38	5,238.76
Net profit		27.2	55.4	39.7

Source: Business Interventions

NOTES

1 Modified from SFr100,000 in accordance with EC Guidelines, from 1 October 1992.
2 Beatrice Engstrom-Bondy and Claire Makin, *Swiss Banking in the 1990s*, London, 1991.

5

EUROPEAN PROFILES II

LUXEMBOURG

The Grand Duchy of Luxembourg has become a renowned international financial centre in the last 30 years. Financial institutions contribute significantly to the GDP and employ approximately 10 per cent of the workforce.

The Duchy's banking tradition, however, goes back to 1856 when the two oldest credit institutions were founded. After the First World War, Luxembourg joined the Belgium Luxembourg Union; in 1929, it created its stock exchange (which, later on, became important with the development of Eurobond business), and passed a law on holding companies, which later attracted many multinationals. In 1945, the Banking Control Act allowed orderly development of banking.

In 1960, there were 15 banks. There are now 218 banks worldwide eligible to operate in the Duchy (some 73 of which were established in the past five years). There are 1,069 established investment funds in Luxembourg with combined net assets totalling more than LFr7,830 billion at the end of the first quarter of 1993, compared to LFr168.4 billion in 1981. This represents a compound annual growth rate of greater than 37 per cent for the period.

Banking environment

Luxembourg originally developed as a centre specialising in diversified portfolios in different currencies. It has traditionally appealed to continental investors who wanted to keep investments offshore and for whom Luxembourg's financial district was within easy reach.

Situated centrally within the European Community, Luxembourg's population is skilled linguistically and in dealing with international currencies. The Duchy enjoys political and social stability. It also maintains a flexible legal framework with strict banking controls, recently reinforced by the law of 5 April 1993, to ensure maximum protection for banking institutions' customers. In addition, Luxembourg maintains Swiss-like banking secrecy laws.

The Luxembourg financial market in retrospect

The financial market in Luxembourg may be said to have been founded in 1856 when the first two credit institutions were established. Subsequently these institutions, and others which followed, initially catered for the needs of the local economy as it transformed itself from a wholly agrarian base to one with a major, and continuously growing industrial component. Internationalisation of the banking sector began in the 1950s and coincided with major political developments in Europe such as the establishment of the European Coal and Steel Community and the signing of the Treaty of Rome, events which laid the foundations of the modern European Community.

The 1960s saw exponential growth and further internationalisation of the financial market as the development of the Eurobond and Eurocurrency markets persuaded major international banks that they required a presence in Luxembourg. Since then Luxembourg has evolved into an important financial centre and over the past few years the emphasis has shifted in favour of private banking, mutual fund and fee-earning business generally.

Despite recent competition from newer offshore banking centres, Luxembourg has been able to maintain its growth rates and continues to develop the expertise gained over the past 30 years.

Table 5.1 Growth in the number of banks, 1970–93

	1970	1980	1985	1990	1992	1993
Luxembourg and Belgium	14	12	12	22	24	25
Germany	3	29	29	38	63	67
United States	7	11	11	12	10	10
France	4	6	7	20	21	21
Italy	—	5	8	11	15	16
Japan	—	4	6	9	9	9
Scandinavia	—	14	16	20	23	19
Switzerland	4	7	7	16	17	17
Other countries	2	12	16	24	28	32
Multinational joint ventures	3	11	6	5	3	2
Total	37	111	118	177	213	218

Source: ABBL

Already the leading European centre for the registration of investment funds, Luxembourg has been swift to develop financial products for the private banking client. Adoption of EC legislation on Undertakings for Collective Investment in Transferable Securities (UCITS), for example, has allowed investment funds to be sold to residents of other EC countries. Some 1,069 investment funds were registered by 1993, of which 848 qualify as UCITS. Most of the funds in private banking accounts in Luxembourg are either held in numbered accounts or in the names of offshore companies (trusts or private investment companies).

Trusts exist subject to the rights of legal heirs being upheld. As a reaction to the greatly increased use of trusts in international private banking, Luxembourg introduced a form of civil law trust relating to fiduciary contracts in 1983.

Holding companies

Assets can be lodged in a holding company, a frequently convenient vehicle for family-owned investments. The shares can be allocated to family members with arrangements to ensure control and continuity. Under Luxembourg law, the activity of holding companies is restricted to the administration of financial assets. This excludes real estate, although shares in companies owning real estate may be held. To protect confidentiality, directors and auditors can be provided. Banks may also provide administration services.

No tax applies to the proceeds of liquidation and no inheritance tax is payable in Luxembourg by heirs of non-resident shareholders.

Trusts

As in Switzerland, Liechtenstein, the Channel Isles and other so-called offshore centres, trusts have an important role to play in wealth preservation, and banks and consultancy companies in Luxembourg have long-standing experience of setting up trusts for customers.

Taxation

There is no withholding tax on interest and dividends received from holding companies and SICAVs (Collective Investment Companies with Variable Capital). Transfers of funds and exchange transactions as well as the purchase and sale of securities are totally free of tax/duties. There is no value added tax on the purchase or sale of gold.

Capital gains realised on the disposal of securities are tax-free for individuals who are non-residents, while residents must have held their securities for a minimum period of six months to benefit from this exemption.

Moveable assets belonging to non-residents are transferable without estate duties being collected in Luxembourg after their death. However, death duties must be paid on real estate located in Luxembourg independent of whether the owner was a resident or not.

Secrecy

Luxembourg bankers wish to retain their competitive edge in a harmonised European Community. Legislation has been introduced to counter money laundering and insider trading. New legislation in line with EC rules will allow bankers freedom from secrecy requirements in cases of suspected money laundering.

Luxembourg continues to resist EC pressure for changes to banking secrecy and tax exemption for non-resident investors. Luxembourg bankers are under no obligation to proceed with EC investigations which conflict with Luxembourg common practice or law under Article 4 of the 1979 Grand Ducal Regulation. European Member States' requests for information can be declined on the basis of the 1989 Grand Ducal Decree of 24 March 1989, which prohibits tax authorities from seeking confidential information on banking clients.

The Luxembourg Law of 5 April 1993 reinforced the bankers' secrecy duty. Its Article 41 (1) provides that the members of the board of directors, the management and other employees of credit institutions are bound to keep confidential all information entrusted to them in the course of their professional activity. Disclosure of such information should be punished according to penalties defined by Article 458 of the penal code.

Therefore, bankers are bound to keep confidential all information entrusted to them in the course of executing their office. The duty of secrecy ceases when disclosure of information is authorised or imposed under law, such as would be the case if the banker is called to testify in court or face imprisonment.

Deposit guarantee scheme

All credit institutions dealing in the private banking sector in the Grand Duchy of Luxembourg became members of a non-profit-making association, the 'Association for the Guarantee of Deposits, Luxembourg'. Affiliation to this Association is a prerequisite for new credit institutions to receive authorisation to operate in the Grand Duchy by local authorities.

This system mutually guarantees the deposits of individuals between members of the Association without distinction of the nationality or residence of these individuals. The guarantee payment is limited to a maximum of LFr500,000 by customer and by credit institution. Corporate entities are excluded from the scheme.

Typical products in the Luxembourg private banking stable include:

Deposits

Interest earned on deposits reflects competitive market rates and is commensurate with amount and maturity. Multicurrency accounts, whereby deposits in different currencies are maintained in one account with valuations in the customer's base currency, are widely offered. No withholding tax applies and arrangements can be made to reinvest deposits automatically at maturity.

Deposits from individuals are guaranteed to a maximum of LFr500,000 by the Luxembourg Association for the Guarantee of Deposits (AGDL).

Fixed income

The financial centre has a wide-ranging capability in the fixed income area. Luxembourg is a prime location for Eurobonds, and the banks are active in all major fixed income markets.

Equities

Transactions are conducted regularly and extensively on the major stock exchanges.

Derivatives

Options and futures are widely used to enhance and/or hedge portfolio investments.

Investment funds

Bankers in Luxembourg arrange investments in various types of investment funds and particularly in umbrella funds.

Custodial services

Full custodial services are supplied, including the regular valuation of portfolios, surveillance of maturities, the collection of coupons and all operations such as stock splits, reimbursements and drawings. A number of banks offer safe-deposit box facilities.

Loans

Investors can normally obtain loans at competitive rates, with minimal formalities, against their deposits and securities. Loans are also available for the purchase of securities on margin account and foreign exchange trading.

The competitive edge

Luxembourg bankers argue that they have a significant competitive edge in their private banking services. The size of the country, its proximity to EC officials and its considerable lobbying skills all mean that Luxembourg can act very swiftly to take advantage of new regulations, new trends and new customer requirements. Its multicultural, almost hybrid style and a general availability of multinational expertise make Luxembourg a leading innovator in the development of service and products.

Luxembourg's private clients may not be the extremely wealthy: nevertheless, there are enough clients of significant wealth to ensure the centre's continuation as a leading financial services provider.

A significant advantage has accrued to the tiny country with the advent of the German withholding tax. The growing competition for German savings coming from international investment fund managers based in Luxembourg is forcing the pace of change in Germany's financial centres. Younger private investors are ignoring the traditional savings methods of the post-war generation and placing money abroad.

German households traditionally placed by far the largest proportion of savings either directly into Deutschemark government bonds or into insurance and pension schemes – whose own policies favoured these same investments. However, a tax introduced by the Bonn government in the late 1980s deducted a portion of dividend income at source. Then on 1 January 1993, Bonn introduced a 30 per cent withholding tax for domestic residents, which sparked a renewed and much bigger exodus of monies from Germany.

According to a study by Deutsche Bank, the number of mutual funds registered in the Grand Duchy rose to 1,175 in 1993 from 1,041 in 1992. Money under management soared to DM480bn ($280bn) from DM320bn. Of the total Luxembourg fund volume, 29 per cent came from Germany and Switzerland, another 8 per cent from France, 6 per cent from the US and 5 per cent from Belgium. In total, money from 23 countries was invested in Luxembourg funds.

The growth in mutual funds registered in the Grand Duchy is driven by several factors. Apart from their invisibility to German tax authorities seeking to collect the withholding tax, they avoid the long-standing German law requiring full tax liability if capital gains are made within a six-month period. Share investment primarily seeks capital gains, which means that it imposes obstacles on investment managers needing the flexibility to take gains for growth whenever they see fit.

Companies such as US-based Fidelity Investment have seen interest in their Luxembourg mutual fund soar. It and others, such as the UK's Robert Fleming group and the US Templeton group, compete with the German banks to offer 'umbrella funds'. These allow investors to switch – at a low or no fee – between different kinds of funds with a focus on a different geographical area.

Funds collected by Templeton's German clients soared by 310 per cent in 1993. Fidelity Investments' funds under management in Europe grew, in 14 months, from the equivalent of $600m to nearly $3bn. Around 40 per cent of this came from German private investors. The changing investment attitude of the average German saver has been the main reason for the growing success of the funds, particularly among younger investors, who expect more sophisticated performance.

Smaller companies are also seeking a foothold in the market. Nestor Investment Management, partially owned by Hamburg's M. M. Warburg, was registered in December 1993 in Luxembourg, but is substantially managed from Germany. Nestor's umbrella fund, which focuses on four geographical regions, including Europe, is designed to capitalise on the growing private and institutional interest from Germany.

Most banks, including the large German ones, offer 'umbrella funds' from Luxembourg which are not liable to German tax and regulatory laws restricting their freedom of movement. Bankers say that the more aggressive focus of foreign funds on achieving better performance has been an attractive sales advantage. It is a growing cause of concern for major German banks such as Deutsche Bank. This will force German banks to become more aggressive and flexible in their investment methods and more transparent and marketing-oriented in presenting different investment alternatives to what has essentially been a captive German market.

Deutsche's Luxembourg subsidiary, the largest bank in the Grand Duchy, reported the highest profits in its 24-year history in 1993 as a result of the new enthusiasm for offshore funds. The number of private customers in the Luxembourg bank rose by 28 per cent in 1993 to 18,000 while the number of accounts more than doubled to 12,000. This also doubled the amount of funds under management to DM5.8bn.

Table 5.2 Luxembourg's share in the external assets and liabilities of the banks reporting to the BIS, 1975–92

	1975	1980	1985	1992
Total in %				
Assets	9.5	11.6	9.5	12.8
Liabilities	9.0	10.4	8.1	10.5
Non-bank sector in %				
Assets	21.3	23.3	17.4	18.5
Liabilities	10.3	9.6	8.1	17.1

Source: ABBL
Note: the reporting zone includes the following countries: Belgium, France, Germany, Italy, Luxembourg, Netherlands, Sweden, Switzerland, United Kingdom; since 1977, Austria, Denmark, Ireland; and since 1983, Finland, Norway and Spain

Tble 5.3 Luxembourg investment funds, 1982–93

| | 1982 | | 1987 | | 1993 | |
	Number	Total assets	Number	Total assets	Number	Total assets
Mutual funds	45	125	124	531	534	6,106
SICAVs*	—	—	222	442	600	3,727
Other funds	42	64	59	162	41	134
Total	87	189	405	1,135	1,175	9,967

Source: ABBL
Note: *société d'investissement à capital variable (open-ended investment fund)

THE CHANNEL ISLANDS – JERSEY

One of the keys for continued success as an international finance centre is stability and future security.

Jersey has the advantage of being able to provide evidence of stability through 30 years of experience during which time there has developed a wide range of financial services of a high standard supported by a labour force with appropriate skills and experience.

For the future, the Island is secure in its relationship with Europe, secure in its status as an international finance centre of the highest reputation and secure in the commitment of the authorities to support the industry.

The above statement is drawn from the *States of Jersey Strategic Policy Report* and reflects the attitude of the Island to defending and developing its long-established reputation of political and fiscal stability.

The financial sector of the Channel Islands has grown significantly in the past few decades and now contributes about half of the national income and employs approximately one-fifth of the labour force.

Current economic statistics show the Island's GDP at £1,285 million in 1991. Jersey has no public debt and had a strategic reserve of £178 million at the end of 1992. Additionally, Jersey has been awarded the Standard and Poor's 'AAA' sovereign rating ceilings for debt obligations of issuers.

The Island's relationship with the European Community is defined by a Protocol attached to the Treaty of Accession of the United Kingdom to the Community. Jersey is neither a separate Member State nor an associate member of the Community. Community directives, existing or proposed, relating to fiscal harmonisation or exchange of information do not apply.

Banking environment

Although the Island issues its own notes and coins, it maintains monetary union with the United Kingdom and benefits from the free flow of capital throughout the European Community and beyond. There is no question of exchange controls being applied to the movement of funds into or out of the Island.

Private banking, investment management, private trusts and global asset protection for wealthy individuals are areas of business that may be undertaken in Jersey on a no tax or low tax basis. There are no higher rates of income tax (or surtax), no capital gains taxes, no estate or inheritance duties and no value added tax. Resident individuals and corporations have been chargeable to income tax at 20 per cent since 1940, but high thresholds result in many individuals paying no tax. The Island's economic policies are directed at maintaining its position on taxation.

Table 5.4 Jersey's national income: two decades of change, 1971–91

	1971 (reflated to 1991 values) %	1991 %
Financial services	15	47
Investment holding	25	19
Tourism	45	27
Agriculture	8	5
Light industry	7	2
Total	£527m	£1,285m

Source: States of Jersey

Over the years Jersey has developed an unrivalled reputation for quality which is based on controlling the banks allowed to operate there. It is interesting to note that when BCCI sought a licence in the early 1980s, it was refused by the local authorities.

There are currently 70 deposit-taking institutions registered under the Banking Business Law and these held deposits of £52 billion at the end of 1993, of which almost 60 per cent was in foreign currencies. All banks operating in the Island are licensed and supervised under the Banking Business (Jersey) Law 1991, and it is the general policy to admit deposit-taking institutions from within the world's top 100 by reference to size of capital base. Banks from 17 different countries are represented.

The 1992 annual review of profits and staff levels of the major financial institutions in Jersey showed an overall increase in profitability of 9 per cent (see Table 5.6).

Table 5.5 Registered banking businesses in Jersey, April 1994

Country	No. of institutions	No. of branches	No. of subsidiaries	Total
Australia	2	1	2	3
Belgium	1	0	1	1
Canada	3	0	3	3
Eire	2	0	2	2
France	2	1	1	2
Germany	2	0	2	2
India	1	1	0	1
Israel	1	0	1	1
Luxembourg	1	1	0	1
Netherlands	1	1	1	2
South Africa	2	1	1	2
Spain	1	0	1	1
Sweden	1	1	0	1
Switzerland	3	4	2	6
United Arab Emirates	1	1	0	1
United Kingdom	18	12	23	35
United States	5	6	3	9
Total	47	30	43	73

Notes:
Branches and agencies   30
Subsidiaries   43
Institutions represented in Jersey   47
Source: States of Jersey Financial Services, 1994

Table 5.6 Profitability of Jersey financial institutions

	Increase/decrease in profits 1991/2	Increase/decrease in staff 1991/2
Banking, business, law institutions	+11.1	−5.0
Trust and company administrators	+5.9	−6.9
Fund management companies	−12.4	−1.8
Accountancy firms	+8.5	−1.9
Total	+9.4	−4.5

Source: States of Jersey Financial Service, 1994

Banks engaged mainly in offshore business averaged profit growth of 15 per cent, with 5 per cent less staff, and average profit per employee increased by 20 per cent to £116,300 in 1992. Bank deposits in March 1993 totalled £54.4 billion, in comparison with Guernsey's £30.3 billion, Gibraltar with £3 billion and the Isle of Man with £2.5 billion. The equivalent of £32 billion of the total was in non-sterling currency deposits. Taken together with the value of assets under administration with trust companies, totalling more than £50 billion, the Island's finance sector can be seen to be handling business worth more than £100 billion.

Table 5.7 Sources of finance sector business

Source of deposit	Total £	%
Interbank market	19,836,595	37.5
Customers	33,078,017	62.5

Source: States of Jersey Financial Services, 1994

Table 5.8 Distribution of investment by region

Residence of depositors	Sterling	Currency	Total
Jersey resident	3,127,621	1,668,015	4,795,636
Jersey financial intermediaries	2,196,497	1,384,968	3,581,465
UK, Guernsey and Isle of Man, unallocated	10,579,683	8,144,446	18,904,129
Other EC members	1,373,347	3,472,701	4,846,048
European non-EC members	894,983	7,186,001	8,080,984
Middle East	623,396	1,976,873	2,600,269
Far East	538,960	2,126,224	2,665,184
North America	549,815	2,509,203	3,059,018
Others, unallocated	2,270,525	2,111,354	4,381,879
Total deposits	22,334,827	30,579,785	52,914,612

Source: States of Jersey Financial Services, 1994

Collective investments

The Collective Investment Funds (Jersey) Law 1988 is the statute under which the Island exercises a regulatory role over mutual funds like unit trusts and open ended companies. This legislation is designed to protect investors in such schemes established in or managed from Jersey and this is achieved by licensing and regulating all the Jersey functionaries of any mutual fund, wherever established.

A record £18.3 billion – an increase of 16.3 per cent over the previous six months – was invested in Jersey collective investment funds as at 30 June 1993, held within 759 separate investment pools.

Jersey trusts

The Trust (Jersey) Law 1984 provides the statutory base for the establishment and operation of trusts on the Island and deals with the duties and responsibilities of trustees as well as the rights of beneficiaries. There is no registration scheme under the law for either individual trusts or trustees although it is planned that the latter will become subject to a licensing and supervision scheme within the next two years. The maximum trust period is 100 years from the date of its creation, and there is no restriction on the accumulation of income.

Trusts established in the Island for the benefit of non-residents are exempt from income tax on overseas income and on bank deposit interest arising in Jersey. They are typically set up for estate planning purposes and for the purpose of deferring or minimising tax elsewhere. Jersey enjoys confidentiality of its banking affairs.

A new vehicle: the International Business Company

Jersey's newest corporate vehicle, the International Business Company (IBC) was introduced in the 1992 Budget, and became available on 1 January 1993. It was created to fill a perceived gap between the exempt company and the standard income tax company. An IBC can be a Jersey incorporated company, a foreign company managed and controlled in Jersey, or a Jersey branch of a foreign company. It must not be beneficially owned in any part by a Jersey resident, although it can have a Jersey intermediate holding company. Full disclosure of beneficial ownership must be made to the Financial Services Department, and it must not have been anything other than an IBC in any prior year of assessment.

An IBC is fully resident for tax purposes in Jersey, and thus becomes an important product in the portfolio of the private banker. It pays tax on profits in the normal way, but is subject to special rates of tax on any profits derived from international activities. These are predominantly activities carried on outside Jersey and include:

- inter-company financial activity;
- industrial and commercial activity;
- overseas investment.

The rates of tax applicable to these profits range from 2 per cent down to 0.5 per cent on profits over £10 million. Jersey sourced profits are liable for tax at 20 per cent.

Initially it was thought that the IBC could be used to deal with the Controlled Foreign Companies (CFC) legislation, which is a feature of anti-avoidance legislation in other jurisdictions such as the UK. It was thought that this could be achieved by mingling Jersey source income with income from international activities to achieve an effective rate of tax greater than half of the equivalent UK tax on the same income. The 1993 Budget effectively scuppered that idea by raising the rate of tax required to avoid CFC legislation to three-quarters of the UK rate.

Because the IBC will be resident in Jersey for tax purposes, it will be covered by the UK/Jersey double tax agreement. This makes it particularly suitable as a vehicle for certain investment and activities in the UK, for example to hold the capital or land equity in UK property development projects for non-UK residents.

GERMANY

The private banking market in Germany is largely a domestic one, with some banks seeing only 10 per cent of their client base from outside the country.

The growth of wealthy individuals is described by private bankers as 'the generation of heirs'. Most old fortunes were in practice eliminated or very much diminished after the Second World War, and the creation of the highly successful industrial nation we know as modern Germany has also created new wealth for successful business owners. The founding generations are now in their sixties and seventies, and are concerned with either passing their wealth on, or selling their businesses and managing the proceeds.

A 1988 survey showed that there were some 130,000 Deutschemark millionaires. This figure, gained from statistics on wealth tax, was probably underestimated. The next survey was in 1995, and the expectation was that the number of millionaires would be doubled. According to Trinkhaus & Burkhardt, a Frankfurt private bank, there is particular growth in the number of people involved as fungible investments rise.

Traditional requirements for German private clients were stocks and bond management. However, with growing financial awareness, and the complexity of available techniques, needs have changed. There is a far greater demand for all-encompassing advice: on securities, real estate, estate planning and management.

The profile of clients is also changing: as younger people inherit wealth from their families, they are more open to considering more complex and perhaps more adventurous paths, such as derivatives and foreign exchange products. Typical clients were 55 or older; now there is a substantially younger client base. The withholding tax imposed by the German High Court, which provided Luxembourg with a great increase in German investment funds, has created some problems for German private clients, but more work for their bankers, as they try to manage the effect by maintaining funds offshore. The complexity of managing the time value of money, for example in bonds, has also created more activity.

Geographically, and perhaps logically, the cities of retirement have seen an increased demand for private client services: in Baden-Baden and Munich, for example. German banking has always been competitive, and of course with the banks' direct investment in industry, strong links between owners and bankers are formed. The big three German banks – Deutsche, Commerz and Dresdner – all have growing private bank operations; Dresdner bank's decision to re-create Hardy & Co. Privatbankiers, an old name in a new setting, is indicative of potential in the market.

The effects of reunification are not yet making an impact on German private banking, with the only HINWIs emerging from land speculation; similarly there is very little German private client demand for investment in Central and Eastern Europe.

The German private client relationship can be immediately profitable for the banker, since commission income quickly becomes available. As a result, the requirement for capital investment is even lower than in other European areas, and the returns on equity and assets are very attractive.

The tight linkage between industry and bank also creates considerable leverage between private client and institutional operations: Trinkhaus & Burkhardt, for example, see their three focus areas of private banking, corporate finance and capital markets and treasury each contributing 30–40 per cent to total earnings.

It is clear that German private banking will continue to be a growth area for banks which focus their operations properly. As well as the native banks, many of the larger global banks have designs on the market and some are already seeing burgeoning opportunity. Equally, there is growing competition from private asset managers, some of whom are ex-bankers. Since they have to work with banks to process client transactions this can increase bank business, but as in Switzerland, this category of advisor may present an increasing threat by standing between bank and client.

Given Germany's demographic position, it is evident that there will be an increasing emphasis on estate planning and management, and a building trust business, which is largely embryonic in the country.

FRANCE

Private banking in France has been concentrated on upper-drawer old families, many with connections between the new and old worlds going back to the 1920s and 1930s. Along with legacies protected by the Swiss during the turbulent eighteenth and nineteenth centuries, the growth in wealth in North America prompted much interest in Europe and particularly in Paris. Trips to Europe frequently became marriages between the two continents, and so French wealth has a stable, old-money base. According to 'la banque Morgan', the private banking market is very domestic: 80 per cent or more of the client base in France is French. Unlike the UK, where tax advantages are significant for people with ordinary resident non-domiciled status, French marginal tax rates are high, and there is also a wealth tax. International private clients are therefore likely to be people who have a love of a particular area of France, or who visit frequently; they have their accounts managed elsewhere but need access when in France.

Part of the importance of the domestic market can be explained by the development of the SICAV. Charles de Gaulle, when president, pushed the French people to become popular shareholders and thus the SICAV was born, offering a particular vehicle to encourage shareholding. In the early 1980s the French created in a very short space of time a strong SICAV market, and the mutual funds business is now one of the largest in Europe. The market bubbled in the period 1984–6, and then came the crash of

1987. French interest rates from that time until probably early 1992 continued to increase because of inflationary pressures: rates were around 10–11 per cent. With inflation decreasing to 3 per cent, real rates of return were 6–7 per cent – clearly a good investment given the nervousness of equities post 1987, and an easy case to make to private clients. In addition, government policy allowed interest to be capitalised tax-free, with a rate of only 19 per cent payable on the sale of a SICAV. This naturally encouraged greater, longer-term investments, and tremendous balances were held in SICAVs. Today, Luxembourg is catching up in the SICAV market, but France remains the leader.

A typical portfolio of a French private client would therefore include a hefty SICAV element, although as rates come down, as in other financial centres, there is more movement into bonds, equities and government privatisation issues. Balladur bonds are also attractive. The French government naturally wants their privatisation plans to be successful, and are likely to find ways of making them attractive to private investors who want to buy into French industry.

French private clients are more inclined to invest domestically, although some continue to find Swiss secrecy an attraction and take their custom across the border.

A new trend is to see an increase in 'self-directed investors': clients who like to split their portfolios, and do some self-management. Even so, the 40-something entrepreneur who understands operational risk in their own business is inclined to conservatism where personal assets are concerned.

THE UK

London's place as a centre for a wide variety of financial business makes it an attractive and exciting private banking environment. Even though the site of the embryonic European Central Bank is to be Frankfurt, London continues to provide many benefits to international private clients.

A 1994 industry survey[1] showed that the number of foreign banks operating in London has passed 500 (to 514) for the first time, whereas Frankfurt has 180 and Paris less than 250. Incoming banks from Russia, the Czech Republic and Asia reflect the recognition of the City as having a key role in banking generally. Critical mass of banks and financial institutions support London's position as crucial to global transactions. The City is the top dealing centre for Treasury products: ForeX daily trading volume is more than $300 billion, and 34 per cent of global turnover takes place in London. By comparison, the volume in Germany is $57bn and in Paris $36bn. It also has the biggest turnover of foreign stocks and shares, accounting for roughly half of the $225bn of equity traded in Britain in the third quarter of 1993; London is the largest international fund management centre in the world.

The legal and tax environment is an attractive one: there are no taxes for foreign investors and residents. Some private bankers are concerned that government should continue to support this policy, arguing that the trade and commerce created by visiting international private clients is considerable. The domestic real estate market, though not necessarily wonderful for Joe Public in the early 1990s, is estimated to be valued at $120bn, and there are no restrictions on non-British buyers.

For private bankers themselves, London's status as an international fine art market, and access to top corporate finance centre professionals make the City a natural choice from which to cater to their wealthy clientele. London's history as a private banking centre in some ways parallels that of Switzerland. By the end of the nineteenth century, leading London merchant banks had developed operations for private clients which became the basis for modern relationship banking.

Modern legislation, such as the 1986 Financial Services Act, prevents individuals or firms from setting up as financial advisors without having to satisfy regulatory requirements. Thus the private UK client is reasonably well protected from unscrupulous advisors who simply put up their brass plate. That does not stop wealthy clients from wanting relationships with old-established and well-known 'names' in the banking world: security is naturally a continuing issue. The FSA has provided some private banks with a tricky decision, however: whether to be totally independent in their investment advice for investments provided through insurance products, or to become tied to a specific 'manufacturer'.

Market drivers

According to a 1992 survey,[2] there are a number of market drivers for private banking in the UK.

Population spread

The age spread of the UK population has a clear impact on the market for private banking. The core of UK clients requesting private banking services are drawn from people of 45 years of age and over. The ageing profile of the UK population therefore has a clear and positive impact on the market. Those aged between 45 and 59 had increased from 9.34 million people in 1989 to almost 10.0 million by 1992. This age bracket was forecast to have reached 10.23 million by 1994.

Growth of personal wealth

The rise in personal wealth over the last decade has clearly helped to drive the market ahead. While much personal wealth is tied up in the form of

Table 5.9 UK population by age group, 1989–92: in millions

	15–19	20–24	25–44	45–59	60+	Total
1989	4.07	4.66	16.44	9.34	11.85	46.36
1990	3.90	4.55	16.66	9.42	11.88	46.41
1991	3.70	4.48	16.84	9.50	11.91	46.43
1992	3.52	4.37	16.80	9.80	11.93	46.42

Source: OPCS Government's Actuary's Department Datamonitor

equity within people's homes, there has also been substantial growth in the value of funds available to be saved.

Inheritance tax

The current law governing inheritance taxation has an indirect effect on the timing and spread of personal wealth in the UK. Beneficiaries may receive substantial amounts of cash or other assets; if the beneficiary is a child, the inheritance may be in the form of a trust. In both cases, the private banking institutions compete for the right to handle the client money with a range of other professionals such as accountants and solicitors.

House prices

The rapid growth in house prices during the 1980s provided one of the main spurs to the growth of personal wealth. The average price of a dwelling has one of the most profound effects on the mortgage market, since the proportion of price mortgaged remains relatively stable. However, there is also a superimposed social trend of greater acceptability of credit and debt, and thus the average advance has increased continuously in real terms, even while house prices have fallen. The problems of negative equity are not generally associated with the clients of private banks.

Investor sophistication

The rise in investor sophistication drives the market for private banking in two main ways. Higher investor sophistication means that the proportion of people wishing to handle their financial affairs on their own may have risen. But it also means that the proportion of customers willing to consider private banking facilities will also have increased.

Undoubtedly over the last ten years the market for investment products has seen a significant rise in the level of investor sophistication. The general population has become increasingly aware of investment products in the last decade, with the increasing take-up of employee share ownership schemes and the development of tax-efficient investment vehicles such as

PEPs. The cross-section of the population able to make use of private banking facilities has undoubtedly shown an increased level of understanding of the investment opportunities open to them. However, as the number of products available to them has also grown rapidly during the course of the last decade, the market has become increasingly complicated. The proportion of potential customers that continue to handle all their affairs without recourse to at least some administrative and execution services offered by the private banking sector is therefore likely to have shown little change.

More importantly, the growth in investor sophistication has brought a greater number of people into the lower end of the market who may previously have placed their funds in more straightforward institutions such as building societies or gilts, thereby avoiding an active management of the portfolio. The growth in the private banking market has been partly dependent on the rise in frequency with which customers have been willing to 'churn' their portfolio. The active management of a greater proportion of customer portfolios has boosted the fortune of the private banking market, even with the effects of bear markets. The commission rates achieved represent the difference between profit and loss on a high percentage of some accounts, once the overhead costs are built into the daily running costs of an individual portfolio.

Role of London in global financial market

It is essential for the UK institutions currently operating in the private banking market that London retains its position of pre-eminence, for two reasons.

First, the private banking sector is dependent on the whole range of institutional market-making and investment services that make up the Stock Exchange. If institutional business started to gravitate towards Paris or Frankfurt, it is unlikely that private banking could be sustained on its own.

Second, the very top end of the private banking market, which caters for particularly wealthy individuals, would be very hard hit if individuals, possibly living abroad for much of the year, no longer viewed London as one of the main financial centres. Unlike Switzerland, which has more stringent laws governing banking secrecy, the London market would be left with only one significant competitive advantage, that of tradition and heritage. As a result business would also move away from London.

Growth of expatriate employment

The UK market has benefited particularly over the last 20 years from the growth of UK professionals working abroad, generally free of tax or in countries with significantly lower levels of taxation. A majority of these professionals are likely to have a disposable income in excess of £50,000 and a significant proportion of this is generally available to be saved. The growth in opportunities for expatriate employment has been focused on regions such as the Middle East, the Far East and, to a lesser extent, South or North America.

Concentration of referral channels

The UK private banking market is highly dependent on new business which is referred directly by existing customers or the professionals that come into direct contact with potential clients. These professionals include solicitors, accountants, tax planning specialists and, to a lesser extent, IFAs (Independent Financial Advisors).

Over the last 7–10 years there has been a clear concentration in the primary channels through which new business is most likely to come. As the leading legal and accountancy firms have merged or achieved rapid organic growth the private banks have been able to achieve a sharper focus on institutions with the most suitable client profiles. This has increased the level of competition in the market since fewer firms handling a greater share of new client business makes it difficult for smaller institutions or new entrants to gain referrals.

At the same time, however, many of the private banking institutions have sought to broaden their coverage of potential new business channels by targeting a greater number of legal and accountancy firms, particularly outside London.

Increased levels of administration

The demand for private banking facilities has increased as the management of investment portfolios has become increasingly complex. One feature of this is in the sheer administration of the portfolio, particularly if the individual aims to manage it actively with regular trading. Private banks are able to cater for the administrative needs of the client if they require an execution-only service. Part of the thinking behind such a service is that the client may ultimately require a full discretionary management service. It is obviously better for a bank to have established a strong relationship with the client by providing this service so that any additional services will also be sought from them rather than a rival institution.

The continuing importance of private banking in London underlies the findings of the Coopers & Lybrand/CBI survey of March 1994. For the quarter, the value of fees and commissions continued to increase strongly, a trend expected to continue over the months ahead.

Table 5.10 Gains in fee income 1993 and first quarter 1994

| | 1993 | | | | 1994 | |
	March	June	Sept.	Dec.	March	June
Value of fee, commission income	+32	+3	+38	+53	+51	+51
Value of net interest and investment income	−1	+17	+20	+36	+8	+26

Source: Coopers & Lybrand/CBI/Business Interventions, 1994
Note: percentage balances over previous three months

Table 5.11 Change in fee income and commissions over last quarter of 1993

	Up	Same	Down	Net gain (loss)
Volume of business	44	51	5	39
Value in £ of fee, commisson or premium income	56	39	5	51
Value of net interest, investment or trading income	18	72	10	8
Average commissions, fees, premiums trends	38	57	5	33
Average operating costs per transaction	0	76	24	(24)
Overall profitability	80	8	12	68

Source: Coopers & Lybrand/CBI/Business Interventions, 1994

THE PLAYERS

A selection of major players in the European private banking sector follows. It is not intended to be exhaustive, but rather to indicate the range of banks, their activities and what are described as their operational strengths.

ANZ Grindlays Bank

European offices:
   London, Jersey.
Private banking European Head Office:
   London.
Style and culture:
   An old-established bank with a history in the Indian sub-continent and the Middle East.
Operational strengths:
   Wholly owned subsidiary of ANZ Group Ltd. Strong client base in Middle East and Asia.

Services and products:
  Range, including 'fund of funds'. Discretionary management services for £250k plus; advisory and review for £50k plus. Offshore, trust and estate planning.
History:
  First established in London in 1828.

Bank Sarasin & Co.

European offices:
  Basle, London, Zurich.
Private banking European Head Office:
  Basle.
Style and culture:
  Uses an oak tree as symbol of solidity, loyalty and strength.
Operational strengths:
  Rapid growth in UK. High percentage of Swiss nationals as clients in Switzerland, with around 2,000 client accounts there. Uses economic and political consultants. Major new building in Basle, 1993. Settlement contracted to Royal Bank of Scotland in the UK.
Services and products:
  Universal bank in Switzerland; fund manager in UK. Range of funds. Uses Eurobond market, basically an institutional instrument, for private clients and funds.
History:
  Became a legal entity in 1900, with preceding firms established in 1841.
Philosophy:
  Always seeking a balanced approach and maintaining quality image.

Bankers Trust

European offices:
  London, Channel Islands, France, Germany, Hungary, Ireland, Italy, Luxembourg, Poland, Spain, Switzerland.
Private banking European Head Office:
  London.
Style and culture:
  Forward looking on investment management side; emphasis on understanding and managing risk in private portfolios. International private banking services available since 1978. Emphasis on country teams.
Operational strengths:
  Major global bank, innovative approach. Steady private banking growth over last five years. International (i.e. outside US) client assets under management $10bn.

Services and products:
    Full range. Packaging, and tailored to client requirements.
History:
    Moved from money-centre bank to highly profitable specialist.
Philosophy:
    Recent campaign: 'Hide from risk and you hide from its rewards.'
    Chairman Charles Sanford: 'Our whole enterprise is uniquely dedicated
    to dealing with global risk.'

Chase Manhattan Private Bank[3]

European offices:
    Geneva, London, Jersey, Luxembourg.
Private banking European Head Office:
    Geneva.
Style and culture:
    Client driven organisation, using and leveraging resources of the Chase
    Manhattan Corporation. Private banking viewed as one of six core
    businesses of the corporation. Customised services for individuals with
    $1m and more of liquid assets.
Operational strengths:
    One of the largest private banks. Has $59.5bn in client assets under
    management. Uses global presence. Has a solid reputation, and is seen
    as an old and established bank.
Services and products:
    Full range – portfolio management, trust and estate planning, currency
    management, etc.
History:
    Bank of the Manhattan Company founded 1799. Opened first London
    office in 1887, and in Switzerland in 1968.
Philosophy:
    Make Chase Manhattan the number one choice. Concentrate on client
    focus, teamwork, quality, professionalism and mutual respect.

Citibank

European offices:
    London, Jersey, Geneva, Zurich, Frankfurt, Lausanne, Lugano, Luxem-
    bourg, Marbella, Monte Carlo, Paris.
Private banking European Head Office:
    Zurich.
Style and culture:
    Innovative and entrepreneurial, some would say aggressive. Probably the
    largest non-Swiss private bank. In 1992, 74,000 clients.

Operational strengths:
  Global reach and emphasis on cross-border services. Recovered premium position after difficult years between 1990 and 1992. At end of 1992, total assets under management $75bn, 33 per cent of them serviced in Europe.
Services and products:
  Full range. Includes access to fine art market and some real estate.
History:
  Founded as trust bank in 1840. Established London branch 1902.
Philosophy:
  'Provide comprehensive financial services of the highest quality to clients of substantial means.'

Kleinwort Benson Private Bank

European offices:
  London, Channel Islands, Geneva, Vienna, Brussels, Paris, Frankfurt, Madrid.
Private banking European Head Office:
  London.
Style and culture:
  In 1992, conducted an extensive survey of clients to assess their perception of KB's services and needs. As a result have introduced changes in team approach, with emphasis on service rather than product. Emphasis on continuity of relationship: 'Our people grow grey with their clients.'
Operational strengths:
  Division benefits from Treasury and dealing services, for facilitation of client business and management of private bank Treasury positions. Channel Island business was worth more than KB's overall market evaluation in 1992.
Services and products:
  Full range, including high interest cheque accounts.
History:
  Established as merchant bank in 1792. Consolidation of various investment activities in 1992, bicentenary year.
Philosophy:
  'Our bank is about niceness.'

J. P. Morgan

European offices:
  Brussels, Paris, Frankfurt, Milan, Amsterdam, Madrid, Geneva, Zurich, London.
Private banking European Head Office:
  Paris.

Style and culture:
>The banker's banker. Stability and solidity, recognised by competitiors as exceptionally well managed and with a highly focused strategy. No plans to be a retail bank. Designates itself as a 'firm' with global whole-sale perspective. 'We are trying to avoid what sometimes appear to be interesting diversions into retail business.'

Operational strengths:
>Total assets under management, end 1992 $121bn, of which private client assets $32bn. Mutual fund assets of $10.3bn. One of larger research organisations in investment management, 85 staff researching equity and capital markets. Strong record of performance against industry benchmarks.

Services and products:
>Management investment portfolios: discretionary and advisory.

History:
>Has built business up over 150 years.

Philosophy:
>'Our clients look to us to add advice to the more routine financial services.'

Trinkaus & Burkhardt

European offices:
>Dusseldorf, Baden-Baden, Berlin, Essen, Frankfurt, Hamburg, Munich, Stuttgart, Luxembourg, Zurich.

Private banking European Head Office:
>Dusseldorf.

Style and culture:
>Clients are 90 per cent German domestic; active competitor in competitive market. 'Free-standing' German private bank, strong capital markets performance. Offers funding and credit mechanisms as well as invest-ment management. Expanding real estate business. Characterised by 'expertise'.

Operational strengths:
>Major shareholding belongs to HSBC group; also a limited partnership. Total assets under management end 1993 DM19.7bn, of which private client assets DM13.2bn. Growth in earnings through Luxembourg sub-sidiary in 1992. Berlin branch reached break-even point within two years. Strong research orientation; product sourcing through capital markets section.

Services and products:
>Style of bank and range of services derive their character from specialis-ation and creativity.

History:
Has been a bank since 1785.
Philosophy:
'Management policy receptive to social, economic and technological change, by experience and expertise of staff.'

Warburg Asset Management Private Investors

European offices:
London, Jersey, Zurich, Isle of Man, Luxembourg.
Private banking European Head Office:
London.
Style and culture:
Comprises the well-known Mercury Asset Management name with various 'Warburg' entities. Tradition of personal attention.
Operational strengths:
Part of the S. G. Warburg group, which has capitalisation of around £1bn and employs 5,000 people worldwide. Long experience of managing private client portfolios; group expertise in investment managment and banking. MAM funds under management £49.7bn, end March 1993; private client funds under management – UK clients £1.4bn, international £0.8bn.
Services and products:
Global equity portfolios, balanced mixed portfolios, single and multi-currency bond and cash, specialist funds. Banking services through group.
History:
Long-established group.

Merrill Lynch International Private Bank

European offices:
London, Geneva, Luxembourg, Germany.
Private banking European Head Office:
London.
Style and culture:
Positioned earlier as serving offshore multicurrency investment needs; now an integrated group with private bankers and financial consultants. Growing rapidly in Europe, has recruited 60+ private bankers.
Operational strengths:
International arm of Merrill Lynch's private client group, which has $525bn of client assets.
Services and products:
Multicurrency securities and investment services; offshore banking and trusts, tax and estate planning, portfolio management, etc.

Philosophy:
'Deliver our unique combination of skills to clients.'

Pictet

European offices:
Geneva, London, Zurich, Luxembourg.
Private banking European Head Office:
Geneva.
Style and culture:
Traditional Swiss partnership of seven. Balance between innovation, performance and tradition important.
Operational strengths:
Increasing institutional emphasis; strong research output. No commercial activity, 'specialisation is strength'. Manages international client assets of more than $30 billion.
Services and products:
Range, focused on investment management.
History:
Established 1805. Thomas Jefferson and Albert Gallatin held regular correspondence with the Pictets.
Philosophy:
From generation to generation, through turbulent times, 'our bank has always been able to safeguard the interests of its clients'.

Lombard, Odier

European offices:
Geneva, Zurich, London, Amsterdam, Gibraltar.
Private banking European Head Office:
Geneva.
Style and culture:
Partnership of eight. Proud of history; embracing modern techniques. Encourages younger staff to propose innovations to partners; short decision-making path. Technology important. Portfolio managers' 'dream machine'.
Operational strengths:
Partners have unlimited joint liability. Voluntary compliance with Swiss capital adequacy requirements.
Services and products:
Full range.
History:
Founded 1798, still resident in Geneva building, which has Empire ambience.

Philosophy:
Actions speak louder than words.

Bank Julius Baer & Co.

European offices:
Zurich, London, Geneva, Frankfurt.
Private banking European Head Office:
Zurich.
Style and culture:
Innovative; first Swiss bank to publish AUMS figures. Makes a point of mixing younger and older staff, to match client profiles. Family run.
Operational strengths:
Client assets under management end 1992: SFr33bn; increased by 17 per cent to SFr38.7bn first half of 1993. Strong fund business. Growing emphasis on institutional business and linkages with private banking.
History:
Founded 1890. Changed structure from partnership to corporation in 1975, consolidated in 1980 to Baer Holding. Members of founding family still actively involved.
Philosophy:
Belief in smaller, tightly client-focused company. Some spin-off companies within the group intentionally small enough to foster creative thinking.

Union Bank of Switzerland

European offices:
Zurich, London, Frankfurt, Luxembourg, Madrid, Milan, Monte Carlo, Paris.
Private banking European Head Office:
Zurich.
Style and culture:
Had reputation for military culture, but is moving away from this. Pride in strength and name. Private bank UK clients typically entrepreneurs. Greater client focus with implementation of 'Marketing 2000' concept.
Operational strengths:
The largest of the Swiss Big Three; triple A rating. Global network, focus on integrated operations. Acquisition of Philips & Drew, now UBS Securities.
Services and products:
Full range.
History:
Foundation in 1865.

Philosophy:
  'The group is the source of very considerable financial strength and expertise which supports the interest of private clients.'

Swiss Bank Corporation

European offices:
  Paris, Germany, Italy, Channel Islands, Luxembourg, Monaco, Netherlands, Poland, Spain, Switzerland, London, Edinburgh.
Private banking European Head Office:
  Lugano/Basle.
Style and culture:
  International name and network; community focus in Switzerland.
Operational strengths:
  Second of Swiss Big Three. Strengthened private banking and trust franchise in 1992. End 1992: SFr33bn client assets under management. Strong branding.
Services and products:
  Full range. Universal bank moved into 'Allfinanz' in 1993.
History:
  Formed new private banking group by combining four old-established banks: Adler & Co., Bank Elinger & Co., Ammand Von Ernst & Co., Ferrier Lullin & Cie.
Philosophy:
  Not unique, but unusual. High premium on service.

Crédit Suisse

European offices:
  365 Swiss branches, Vienna, Channel Islands, Paris, Germany, Gibraltar, Isle of Man, Italy, London, Luxembourg, Monaco, Spain.
Private banking European Head Office:
  Geneva.
Style and culture:
  Ranges from staid to aggressive, depending on focus! Available, developing new approaches to private banking. Staff development a key area.
Operational strengths:
  One of the Swiss Big Three. Part of CS Holding, which also incorporates Leu Holding and CS First Boston. Acquired Swiss Volksbank in 1993.
Services and products:
  Full range: delivered through Crédit Suisse, itself, and also Bank Leu and other acquisitions. Major fund manager in Switzerland.

History:
Originated as bank financing tunnel construction in Switzerland. Has become universal bank.
Philosophy:
Recent campaign: 'Incredibly global, incredibly private.' Emphasis on superior service quality.

Coutts & Co.

European offices:
London, Zurich, Channel Islands, Geneva, Cuiasso, Lausanne.
Private banking European Head Office:
Zurich.
Style and culture:
'The Royal Bank'; London operation has frock-coated bankers. History and olde-worlde style belies sharpness and focus in market. Every customer by definition is a private banking customer; derided by competitors as red-carpet retail.
Operational strengths:
Single shareholder is NatWest Bank, with international network and reach. Around 40,000 client accounts in UK; 25,000 internationally.
Services and products:
Up-scale retail products, plus investment/portfolio management.
History:
Celebrated 300-year anniversary in 1992.
Philosophy:
Become first choice for existing and potential clients.

Barclays Private Bank

European offices:
London, Geneva, Lugano, Zurich, Liechtenstein, Channel Islands.
Private banking European Head Office:
London.
Style and culture:
Separate ethos and identity from UK clearer. 'Returning to the business Barclays had before mass personal banking became the norm.' Strong growth in business, staff and presence.
Operational strengths:
Wholly owned by Barclays group, which had a bad 1992 but made considerable strides forward in 1993. Uses BZW for portfolio management. Strong presence in continental Europe, particularly France and Spain (retail banking).

Services and products:
  Full range: discretionary, advisory, cash management. One of top five
  trust providers.
History:
  Barclays origins go back to 1690. Private bank consolidated early 1992.

Table 5.12 European private banking operations by country (not exhaustive)

Switzerland
ABN-AMRO
American Express
ANZ Grindlays
Bank Julius Baer & Cie
Bank Sarasin & Cie
Bank S. G. Warburg Soditic
Banque Bruxelles Lambert
Banque Kleinwort Benson
Barclays Bank
BIL Banque
British Bank of the Middle East
Chase Manhattan Private Bank
Citibank
Coutts & Co.
Crédit Suisse
Darier, Hentsch & Cie
Guyerzeller Bank
Kredietbank
Lloyds Bank
Lombard, Odier & Cie
Merrill Lynch Bank
J. P. Morgan
Pictet & Cie
Paribas
Standard Chartered Bank
Swiss Banking Corporation
Trinkhaus & Burkhardt
UBS

UK
ANZ Grindlays
Bank of Nova Scotia
Bankers Trust
Citicorp
Paine Webber
Kleinwort Benson
Lloyds
Standard Chartered
C. Hoare & Co.
Bank of Scotland
Coutts & Co.

Adam & Co.
United Bank of Kuwait
Central Hispano Bank (UK)
Barings Asset Management
Brown Shipley
Hambros
Hill Samuel
Lazards
N. M. Rothschild
Samuel Montagu & Co.
Schroders
Discount Bank & Trust

Luxembourg
BBL
BNP
Kredietbank
Bank Leu
Banque Privée Edmond de Rothschild
Banque Safra-Luxembourg
State Street Bank Luxembourg

France
J. P. Morgan
Banque Paribas
Crédit Commercial de France (CCF)

Germany
BHF-Bank
Commerzbank
Grunelius KP Privatbankiers
Hardy & Co. Privatbankiers
Trinkhaus & Burkhardt

Liechtenstein
BIL
Neue Bank
Liechtensteinische Landesbank
Verwaltungs-und Privat-Bank
Aktiengesellschaft

Netherlands
ABN-AMRO

Philosophy:
Partnership with clients based on loyal, committed and professional service.

NOTES

1 Noel Alexander survey, March 1994.
2 Datamonitor, Private Banking and Client Services, May 1992.
3 At the time of publication, it is not clear how the merger of Chase Manhattan and Chemical Bank will affect private banking operations.

6

THE INFLUENCE OF
NON-EUROPEAN ACTIVITY

US BANKS IN EUROPE

Globality, pro-activity, risk management: when US banks enter into the European private banking market, these are their watchwords. Do they work? Of course the answer is both yes, and no. In Switzerland, American Express, Security Pacific, Chemical Bank and State Street Bank & Trust either scaled back their operations or pulled out of the market, yet Citibank, Chase Manhattan and Merrill Lynch have stayed the course and are doing well. An assumption that Swiss private clients required global access and highly developed products was not necessarily the correct one. In London, the picture is somewhat different: the City's attractiveness as a financial centre with considerable expertise and innovation contrasts with expectations in Switzerland. There is a private understanding that a high percentage of client wealth preservation is an important part of Switzerland's image, while London attracts rather more clients who are looking for wealth enhancement: the nest-egg versus the gambling stake.

Growth in European market share is a key target, and the larger US banks are typically aggressive in their pursuit of the Euro-HINWI. Merrill Lynch, a firm which has a well-known name in the capital markets, proudly boasts of hiring more than 35 new private bankers in their 1992 annual report; by late 1993 this had risen to 60. More recently in 1993, a team of four bankers was recruited from Lloyds UK private banking operation to join Merrill, whose international private banking group is organised around regional banking centres in London, the Channel Islands, Geneva, the Cayman Islands and New York, with many other office locations.

In continental Europe, J. P. Morgan's long presence in France means that it is equally well known as 'la banque Morgan'. Most of the US banks see growth in Italy, Spain and Germany and are building their presence in these countries. Citibank lays claim to being the largest non-Swiss private bank in the world, with (at the end of 1992) 74,000 clients and assets under management of $75 billion. Of these, 56 per cent are serviced in the US and Latin America, 33 per cent in Europe and 11 per cent in Asia.

J. P. Morgan

Morgan is seen as 'the banker's banker': stable, solid and recognised by competitors as exceptionally well managed and with a highly focused strategy. Designating itself as a 'firm' with a global wholesale perspective, J. P. Morgan has no ambitions to be a retail bank, and does not need to transform its culture from a retail history – unlike many of the bigger banks now trying to enter the private banking market.

In 1992, the bank increased assets under management by $16 billion, bringing the total to $121 billion. Private client assets account for $32 billion of the total. Mutual fund assets grew by 26 per cent in the same period to $10.3 billion. J. P. Morgan continues to place great emphasis on its research capability, with some 85 staff researching equity and capital markets, one of the largest research organisations in investment banking.

The year 1993 was an exceptional one for many banks, and this was certainly the case for Morgan. Earnings for the year were up 53 per cent to $1.7 billion, earnings per share rose to $8.48 (from the previous year's figure of $5.66), and overall return on common stockholder's equity was 22 per cent.

Assets under management in 1993 grew by $26 billion to $147 billion, of which private clients' assets were $39 billion. Mutual funds assets amounted to $13.5 billion, an increase of 31 per cent.

Reliance on capital market expertise and portfolio management ability has played an important part in Morgan's strategy for investors of substantial assets for more than a century. Entrepreneurs and HINWIs – and their families – a typical US bank mix – are offered investment and fiduciary services, managed investment portfolios, and securities brokerage and custody services for clients taking a more active role in their wealth management.

Steadily rising revenues were apparent in 1992 from investment management and operational services provision: fees in both areas grew 17 per cent, and asset management is recognised as one of the faster growing producers of revenue since the mid-1980s. A base of $7 billion of stockholders' equity contributes to Morgan's solid base, and is an obvious consideration for the prudent wealthy individual.

Investment management fees, derived from investment management for institutions and for HINWIs, including administration of trusts and estates, grew from $285 million in 1990, to $321 million in 1991, and to $377 million in 1992; 1993 brought fees up again, to $464 million.

Morgan's European private banking operation is managed out of Paris, where it began offering such services 125 years ago. It is still in the building bought in 1926. Clients are typically traditional upper-drawer, old families, and reflect marriages between wealthy families in Europe and the US in the 1920s and 1930s. Other European operations include Milan, where new mutual funds are growing as part of regulatory and pension changes; Madrid, where the mutual fund business has grown over the last 5–6 years, and the bank has a strong presence, with 3–4 years of private banking onshore business, a growing new area; and Frankfurt, where the business has been established for some 50 years, working with young entrepreneurs building businesses after the last war. Morgan sees a tremendous amount of wealth having been built up, with much industry in private ownership, but little interest in business from second generation inheritors. Although the bank is unlikely to replace the large German family 'house-bank', it has an international window and expects to benefit from the expertise built up over the years.

Typical Morgan clients have large fortunes, of $5 million and more; the bank's strategy is to offer made-to-measure investment management, and so concentrates on significant wealth. Naturally, this implies the international market: families with international connections, even though their wealth may be domestic. In the French market, which is largely domestic, Morgan's description of the private banker is as a combination of family doctor, psychologist, banker and notary; they quote one family relationship where four generations have been clients of the bank. Assets under management in France, which includes institutional business, is between $130 and $150 billion – however, a large percentage of this is said to be institutional and US money.

Morgan is seeing growth in intermediaries in the client relationship – a variety of people such as notaries, lawyers and, in Italy, *commercialistes*. At the same time, there is tremendous growth in funds, which have a cost-efficient execution mechanism from the bank's viewpoint; diversification of client portfolios is increasing, and fine-tuning the asset allocation to provide a strong return has become a crucial part of the investment management process. Private client business has two extremes: great performance, for example the Soros funds, and people who simply 'hang up their shingle' and start operating as a private client advisor. (Interestingly, Morgan's US trust business was sold in January 1994 to a Minneapolis banking group.) The bank expects great changes in Europe as a result of fortunes crossing generations, privatisations and the IPO surge in the US; as wealth gets created and liquefied major opportunities will be presented in Europe over the next five years. A major challenge for the HINWI, from Morgan's viewpoint, is to get through the noise of the many competitive offerings in order to get real quality of service and performance.

Citicorp

The giant Citicorp has played a leading role in the development of the private banking business, identifying the sector early on as having tremendous potential, and going aggressively after market share. Its global franchise and network have facilitated development of the private client service, now regarded as 'a significant growth franchise'. The bank is organised into a Global Consumer business and a Global Finance business, and private banking is part of the former. An indication of the bank's increasing focus on the sector is its inclusion in annual reports, a clear change from the end of the 1980s.

Private bank revenue in 1993 grew from $0.8 billion to $1.0 billion. (By comparison, the other Global Consumer sectors contributed joint revenue of $9.9 billion: $5.3 billion for cards and $4.6 billion for branch banking.) Overall, Europe's revenue for all consumer business was $2.0 billion.

The private bank's results show a 19 per cent growth in revenues, with an earnings increase of more than 50 per cent. The ROA (Return on Assets) was a very solid 1.85 per cent, by comparison with the overall global consumer ROA of between 0.89 per cent (North America, Europe and Japan) and 2.22 per cent (developing economies). The bank sharpened its strategic and operational focus on delivering wealth management benefits during the year.

Table 6.1 Citicorp asset and equity returns, 1989–93

	1993	1992	1991	1990	1989
Overall bank					
Return on total assets	0.84%	0.32%	(0.41%)	0.14%	0.23%
Return on common stockholders' equity	17.7%	6.5%	(14.3%)	2.1%	4.3%
Global Consumer					
North America, Europe and Japan	0.89%	0.52%			
Developing economies	2.22%	2.13%			

Source: Citicorp *Annual Reports*/Business Interventions

Citibank's Swiss operation is the sixth largest private bank, and largest foreign bank, in Switzerland. It has 87 private banking offices in 31 countries, and claims 75,000 clients worldwide. This is an increase of 1,000 on 1992, which in itself was a 5 per cent increase on the previous year; average level of assets under management at that stage was $1m per client, although this does not match the bank's current move towards very high net worth individuals in its European operation.

The private banking operation recognised some years ago its need to move from a service culture – which of course remains a key element of managing clients' wealth – to a more pro-active sales and service environment, and it developed a range of tools and techniques to support staff in doing so. Major effort went into consolidating client information across the world, towards the provision of an integrated statement; hi-tech products were developed to model client profile and investment objectives against bank offerings, along with cross-selling opportunities, and improving the productivity of each member of a private banking team was a high priority.

Citibank Private Bank saw increases in revenues and earnings during 1993; substantial investment management and derivatives products activity in the European private banking business contributed to offsetting competitive pressures in the competitive US credit card market, lower loan volumes in the US branch business, and the impact of non-strategic business dispositions. Global Consumer's overall revenue for 1993 grew by a modest 3 per cent.

Citibank Global Asset Management (CGAM) works with both sectors, Global Consumer and Global Finance, in providing investment management products and services – and includes mutual fund customers. Specialised investment products attracted in excess of $1 billion of client funds in 1993: venture capital for private clients is a growing sector in Europe. Although financial results are included in both Global Consumer and Global Finance figures, CGAM expanded rapidly during 1993, with assets under management and advice growing to $74 billion. In 1992, the total of $66 billion was split between institutional assets of $35 billion, and $25.4 billion for private clients; a further $5.6 billion of assets was for retail clients. Assets of mutual funds offered by the private bank around the world were approximately $4 billion.

Future focus areas include onshore banking in some of the larger European countries, for example France and Italy. According to Citi marketeers, the owners of smaller and medium sized fortunes are becoming more international in their outlook, which gives new opportunity for the bank. London business continues to grow, and has seen recent developments in property and the art market.

ASIA PACIFIC AND LATIN AMERICA

With their global reach, and their emphasis on products and performance, the US banks providing private banking are attractive to those accumulating wealth in the Asia Pacific and Latin American regions.

For Bankers Trust, although Asia, Europe, the Middle East and Latin America all currently contribute similarly to operations, there is more growth in Latin America than in other regions. Citibank is seeing huge growth in Asia Pacific, which is managed from their Singapore base. European banks, too, are focusing concerted effort in these areas: Crédit Suisse has a large unit concentrating on Latin America, Barclays senior managers have trips to Brazil on their itinerary, and naturally the HSBC group, with its history and presence in South East Asia, is increasing the number of its clients in Asia generally.

Chase Manhattan's research found that 15 per cent of offshore wealth emanated from Latin America, and an equal 15 per cent from Asia. With the Middle East also contributing 15 per cent, the growth potential in the opposing geographies is evident. Chase currently put the size of the market at $0.35 trillion in Latin America, and $0.65 trillion in Asia Pacific, with rapid growth foreseen. In 1992, Citibank saw a return on equity of 39 per cent for their total operations in developing economies, and estimate that a 16 per cent growth rate in revenue is achievable over the next five years. (When set against OECD figures of 9 per cent ROE (Return on Equity), and 8 per cent growth in revenue, it is clear where the greater profitability exists.) Investment in the regions, whether by nationals or foreign investors, is also growing.

Citibank's Global Asset Management (CGAM) laid claim to over $2 billion in emerging markets assets under management in 1992, which amounted to 3 per cent of their total figure. Of J. P. Morgan's reported foreign country related assets of $43,165 million, 4 per cent ($4,615m) is attributed to Asia Pacific, and $5,062m, or 5 per cent, to Western Hemisphere excluding the United States. Bankers Trust's Global Emerging Markets sector provides merchant banking products and services in Latin America, Asia, the Middle East and Africa; interestingly the bank finds that Latin Americans are not interested in Asian investment, and vice versa, although both sides are beginning to find Central and Eastern Europe, and Israel, interesting areas for investment.

US PRIVATE BANKS: A CHALLENGING BUSINESS BY COMPARISON

In November 1993, the American Bankers Association (ABA) published the results of a survey of American private bankers carried out by Dartmouth

Table 6.2 Selected private bank presence in Latin America and the Asia Pacific rim

Bank	Latin America	Asia
Bankers Trust	Argentina, Brazil, Chile, Colombia, Antilles, Puerto Rico, Venezuela	Australia, Hong Kong, Indonesia, Japan, New Zealand, Philippines, Thailand, Singapore
Citibank	Argentina, Brazil, Venezuela, Mexico, Chile	Indonesia, Philippines, Seoul, Hong Kong, Japan, Singapore, Thailand, Australia
Merrill Lynch	Argentina, Brazil, Chile, Puerto Rico, Panama, Venezuela, Uruguay	Australia, Hong Kong, Taiwan, Thailand
J. P. Morgan	São Paulo, Rio de Janeiro, Buenos Aires, Caracas, Mexico	Tokyo, Hong Kong, Jakarta, Manila, Australia, Seoul, Taipei
Crédit Suisse	Argentina, Brazil, Chile, Colombia, Mexico, Uruguay, Venezuela	Australia, China, Hong Kong, Japan, Korea, Singapore, Taiwan
Swiss Bank Corp.	Argentina, Brazil, Chile, Colombia, Ecuador, Mexico, Panama, Peru, Uruguay, Venezuela	China, Hong Kong, India, Japan, Singapore, South Korea, Taiwan, Thailand
UBS	Colombia, Brazil, Argentina, Venezuela, Mexico	Japan, China, Hong Kong, Australia, Taiwan
Barclays	N/A	Hong Kong, Tokyo
Coutts & Co.	Uruguay	Hong Kong, Japan, Singapore

Source: Business Interventions, 1993

Research Company, and addressed to attendees at the ABA Private Banking Symposium. Its findings were surprising. Designed to identify private banking concerns when applying technology to strategic thinking, the survey uncovered a range of nervousness in respect of the inability to capture total relationships and profitability, a lack of global processing and accounting capabilities, limits to productivity, an absence of management information tools, and the impact of technology – or its lack – as detrimental to competitive position.

It is clear that the market in America is markedly different from that in Europe; American clients expect extremely sophisticated products as well as high performance, and the American private client is likely to be far more product-oriented, while also expecting a high degree of service. However, what happens in America tends to reach Europe sooner or later, and European private banks will do well to consider the concerns expressed as an early indication of impact to come.

When asked to rank sources of new business, private banking institutions asserted that existing clients were their primary source, as indicated by 84 per cent of all responses. European private banks interviewed for this publication have indicated that client referral is a primary source for them, too. Asked to rank key factors that promote the offering of new products and services, 60 per cent of the US respondents indicated that client requests and competitive offerings were the top two influences.

The inference is clear: if private banks wish to continue to be as responsive to their client needs as they can, and yet compete with rival offerings, they must focus more attention on techniques and technology that allows them to do so. Key issues are cost containment, followed by product innovation and technology. Re-engineering of business processes is one method which caught US bankers' interest, along with workflow management, automation for the sales force, and the leading topic of interest, marketing databases and database management. European bankers will do well to consider techniques such as fast cycle time improvements, re-engineering and overall strategic alignment now, rather than waiting for the trend to trickle across the Atlantic.

Concerns with existing and new technology

A cumulative list of concerns with existing technology in private banking organisations emphasised the following in the ABA survey.

Cannot get a true picture of profitability

This is a common problem, reflecting banks' long overdue need to account for both client and product profitability. Breaking down a complex investment advice package into product profitability is much needed, but difficult even to contemplate for many private banking operations.

Unable to obtain management reports on the business

The importance of effective technology cannot be emphasised enough.

Not able to improve or measure customer profitability

The larger, more successful banks have a clear strategy of 'weeding out' clients who do not provide them with a good level of profit.

Cannot track the total relationship and profitability

Interestingly, this relates to the problems many banks are experiencing in operating on a continent-wide or international basis, where account-responsible officers have conflicting goals which demand they claim ownership for business booked. Double accounting is a problem receiving much attention.

Failure to capture re-engineering opportunities

The inherent stability of private banking impedes progress in this regard, specifically in product development and time to market.

Limited productivity

This is directly related to failure to capture opportunities for re-engineering.

Current systems do not support cross-selling

Integration of client information is a prerequisite for cross-selling.
  For new technology, these were some of the primary issues:

- lack of awareness of what technology is available;
- no knowledge of whether technology would improve client service;
- getting timely information to the decision-makers is problematic;
- benefits and longevity of the system are difficult to assess;
- training is imperative for keeping up with advances in technology;
- cost effectiveness is difficult to assess.

Changes foreseen

When asked to list the top three changes in client needs respondents see in their private banking business over the next two years, many replies emphasised product offerings versus customer needs. Responses predict the following:
- too many suppliers;
- a younger and more performance-oriented clientele;

- access to other firms' products through established banking relationships;
- greater demand for efficient service;
- real-time reporting capabilities.

Posit these predictions against an 88 per cent expectation that the total number of new private banking accounts are forecasted to be greater than the previous year, and similarly new assets for deposit in private banking, and it becomes apparent that service and product lifecycles must be considerably shortened to maintain competitive positions. Since private banking relies on service relationships, the growth in business will require greater management focus as staffing increases, and close attention to the cost of client acquisition and client profitability.

Table 6.3 Operating revenues: net interest income v. non-interest revenues. Top 15 US banks ranked by proportion on non-interest revenues to total operating revenues

1993 first half	Net interest income	Non-interest revenues	Fee revenue	Trading revenue
Bankers Trust	29%	71%	37%	34%
J. P. Morgan	32%	68%	34%	34%
First Chicago	39%	61%	52%	9%
Citicorp	48%	52%	39%	13%
Chemical Bank	57%	43%	30%	13%
Chase Manhattan	59%	41%	29%	12%
Fleet Financial	64%	36%		
BankAmerica	64%	36%	30%	6%
Norwest	64%	36%		
First Interstate	69%	31%		
NationsBank	70%	30%		
Wells Fargo	71%	29%		
PNC Financial	72%	28%		
First Union	73%	27%		
Banc One	75%	25%		

Source: Keefe, Bruyette and Woods, 1993
Note: non-interest revenue broken down by fee and trading components where significant

A survey in March 1993 of 45 bankers from 21 American states provided a snapshot of the private banking business, as well as private bankers' views of the future.[1] The surveyed bankers had different definitions of private banking: 52 per cent said the label covered any products marketed to the affluent, 39 per cent said it covered retail credit and deposit products, and 23 per cent used the term to describe trust and investment products. Measuring profitability was a top priority, and a very critical measurement. Those without performance measurements are developing them now.

Private bankers surveyed said they would like to be able to calculate the profitability of products, accounts, relationships and their staffs. They also want to measure the costs of winning new customers. With those data, they would like to compare their institutions with other private banks – especially those considered highly profitable. Those who do calculate division profitability lack confidence in their ability to maintain current profitability, according to the study. The average private bank, as developed from survey responses, has 4,950 accounts. Each relationship officer had an average of 75 clients.

The typical American client has a net worth of $2.3 million and an income of $270,000, although 29 per cent of the respondents had no minimum net worth criteria. The average loan is $550,000 with a three-year term. In terms of minimums, the average minimum loan is $125,000, the average minimum deposit $70,000 and the average minimum investment account $300,000.

While loans are still a major component of private banking, the surveyed bankers said they should shift their focus from credit to asset management. It was thought that those who are still focusing heavily on credit will fall by the wayside if they do not move toward asset management.

The surveyed banks have private banking units separate from trust and investment groups, but said integrating those businesses is important to improve profitability.

Many respondents said they offer unique services to differentiate themselves from competitors. These included special automated teller machine withdrawal limits, a paging service, collectibles storage, educational forums and real estate advice.

About one-quarter of responding bankers offer international private banking. For them investment management is most important, followed by deposit products and loans. Of those offering international service, half have multilingual staffs. They emphasise frequent personal contact, including one to two trips to the foreign client each year.

Looking to the future, private bankers said that the ability to deliver a high level of service is the most important business factor. Other important issues include: lending money quickly, providing superior investment performance and offering one primary contact for each client.

RISK MANAGEMENT

American influence on risk management is important to private banking, and of course to banking in general. J. P. Morgan's chairman said it thus: 'Risk is there to be managed, not just to be avoided.'[2] Bankers Trust, too, emphasises this approach in their private banking service: clients are questioned carefully and directly in order to understand their risk profile, and to check whether they understand the degree of risk to which they are already exposed. This approach is closely connected to the bank's own risk management strategy.

The growing importance of risk management for leading banks centres around a few American and European commercial banks which, according to an *Economist* survey,[3] are 'spearheading a veritable revolution in risk management that others must one day emulate'. Bankers Trust is a leading proponent of this approach. Citibank's 1992 annual report contains several pages on its new approach to the topic, and Chase Manhattan took an estimated 18 months to reorganise its treasury and trading activities following a risk management audit. The demise of Barings Bank, an institution which many regarded as a stalwart of the UK merchant banks, shows just how important effective risk management is.

As a constant trade-off between volatility and security, asset management must incorporate a stringent attitude to risk management. As *The Economist* survey points out, if a firm were to hedge all its risks, nothing bad would happen to it, but nor could it gain anything. Volatility is the link between risk and reward, and banks must turn that premise to workable business propositions. In its leading-edge stance on risk management, some rivals believe Bankers Trust to be more like a consulting firm than a traditional bank. It is an approach well suited to private banking.

NOTES

1 Survey for *The American Banker*.
2 Interview with *Banking World*, February 1992.
3 A survey of international banking, *The Economist*, April 1993.

7

INTERMEDIARIES AND A NEW COMPETITIVE THRUST

FUND MANAGERS AND INSURANCE PROVIDERS: SETTING THE PACE?

The development of funds as a major product in the private banker's stable has enabled, even encouraged, the growth of a niche: the sourcing of a key product outside the control of the bank. Thus the private banker in his advisory role has become the user of an advisor. At the same time, the development of private client advisory services – through professionals such as lawyers, or by targeted boutiques – has created another set of pressures. While the market certainly has room for a variety of service providers, there may very quickly come a time when these substitute private bank/client services significantly extend to capture a large share of the market.

Recent and ambitious entrants to the private banking market can find that their organisation's global reach and leverage restrain as much as they support. The choice of service or product is perhaps a non-choice: clients may be forced into using the bank's products against their relationship manager's better judgement or recommendations, simply because 'that's what there is'. The more enlightened banks are beginning to buy products from other sources, and this trend is likely to continue as more banks rediscover their core businesses. In theory, and perhaps not so far ahead in practice, a private banking operation could be a very tight, small one: buying in products, research, computing power, property management, and trading and settlement transactions.

The first step in that direction has been taken with the development of specialist fund managers, funds of funds, and managers of fund managers. The trade-off between 'make' or 'buy' is becoming more and more important.

MULTIMANAGERS AND FUNDS

The Wall Street Journal Europe reported in late 1993 on the niche which was becoming a vogue. In London and Switzerland, multimanager funds are attracting interest – not surprising in a low interest rate environment. The basic premise of a multimanager fund is that an investor can place money with well-known professional money managers; the fund then parcels the investment out to money managers around the world. George Soros is one of the pioneers in this market, and few would doubt his ability to create a strong performance.

The use of this technique has considerable attractions for the private investor. For one thing, it provides access to managers who generally only handle money for institutional investors. High returns are possible, as the bigger money managers often use complex instruments, like derivatives.

In America, particularly Miami, new firms known as 'boutiques' are offering a less costly, less regulated way of doing business with wealthy Latin Americans. Many have only a handful of employees, and operate as securities brokers, investment bankers and merchant bankers. The niche they exploit is in providing debt and equity offerings of Latin American companies and governments, rarely available at Miami banks. Since foreign banks are not permitted generally to sell stock and bond products directly in the US, Miami foreign bankers find referral to specialists a better alternative than setting up offshore facilities to sell such products. The specialist boutiques complement private banking activity, and offer a glimpse of another new direction in the industry.

Global Asset Management (GAM) was one of the first European groups to go into the multimanager fund business. GAM was founded by Gilbert De Botton, who at 32 went to work for the Rothschild family, and opened a bank for them in Zurich in the late 1960s. The bank was successful in drawing assets, but like many other houses suffered from not being able to pull all 'the best' portfolio managers under one roof. De Botton's view was that the best talent lies with independent asset managers. In founding GAM he moved from being a money manager to being a manager of money managers. This is how the organisation describes its focus:

> The use of Funds as portfolio sub-components as yet enjoys little acceptance. They are wrongly thought to detract from personalised management, whereas in GAM's view they free the organisation to structure individual portfolios optimally. The management of each of the Funds and in particular the selection of securities is carried out by specialists who, *unfettered by individual client relationships*, can dedicate their time and expertise to chosen markets. The results achieved and the high relative performance of most GAM Funds around the world, in the highly competitive universe in which GAM operates, lend support to the approach. Results are monitored by independent rating institutions and quality is more easily controlled when information must be publicly disclosed.[1]

The company has a good reputation for asset allocation, performance and organisational efficiency; it was recently described by a senior figure in private banking as 'remarkably well organised'.

The idea of sub-contracting top investment talent is not a new one. In 1969 a Geneva-based money management boutique, Notz, Stuckie & Cie, made the first $100m investment in George Soros's now famous Quantum Fund. Quantum went on to record the best sustained performance of any investment fund; the boutique's clients are still invested in it.

The use of this approach embraces many of the principles now becoming more current in organisation management. As a model of the Shamrock Organisation,[2] it requires a tight core team, and careful management of services purchased – the other leaves of the shamrock. De Botton compares himself to a conductor of an orchestra filled with virtuosos.

Multiplus Finance is another example of the emergence of a new style of intermediary. The company was formed to cater for friends of the founders who had difficulties in understanding or following the performances, risks, total costs and quality of execution in their portfolios. In an interview with the journal *Private Banker International*,[3] executive director Fernando de Esconiaza described the firm's development thus:

Instant worldwide communication flows have fostered people's expectations on the amount of information they wish to have on their affairs. They all wanted to have a way of better controlling their assets, see them consolidated, and particularly to obtain more financial transparency. We thus decided to try and help them.

Multiplus has as its clients families, some institutions and other intermediaries like trust lawyers; it can get involved in the choice of appropriate institutions to best attain set objectives for clients. In managing the consolidation of client estates and monitoring and comparing performance, Multiplus has perhaps taken on the original role of the private banker – before poor overall banking performance created an aura of distrust and generated the splitting of clients' total wealth over a range of advisors. Interestingly, these comparisons and consolidation may in the future provide a means of ranking private banks, something not easily achieved at present.

The issue driving Multiplus Finance's success, and perhaps the other niche players also, is the trend towards more price transparency. The switch to fixed management fees, in itself a response to brokerage competition and earnings erosion, permits fund managers to act with more flexibility. Eventually, this will lead to clients having full knowledge of the cost of managing their assets.

Outsourcing is a term more frequently associated with technology and facilities management than with the provision of financial services to a financial services provider. Yet as Margaret Ruffer, of the Belanos Consultancy, points out, it can be a much more cost-effective way of structuring the private bank operation:

Let us consider an example of one of the more expensive areas: fund management. As we know fund managers are expensive creatures, sometimes they do not justify the expense as statistically 50 per cent will be below average at any one time. Fully loaded a fund manager will cost anything from £250,000 upwards. Not only must the bank pay for the salary but also computer systems, information systems such as Oracle, Topic, Reuters, development time, and all the administrative paraphernalia that comes with it, to say nothing of premises, heating, lighting, etc. Furthermore they must have sufficient assets to manage. Do they provide you with a sufficient range of investments to meet your clients' investment needs adequately.[4]

By contracting out everything except asset allocation, strategy and relationship management, the small private bank unit can concentrate on core activity, and coincidentally, provide a meaningful model for the larger operation too.

Private banks of any size cannot afford to ignore the importance of the intermediary, as a threat to their businesses, and as a potential partner. Perhaps they are best termed 'disintermediaries': their giant competitors should watch that disintermediation does not become as much of a *fait accompli* for the private banking sector as it has in retail and corporate banking.

SAVINGS AND INSURANCE PRODUCTS: MOVING FUNDS FROM SAVINGS TO WEALTH

It is clear that commission and fee income are becoming more important for all banks throughout Europe as they come under competitive pressure. Thus was the private banking business born, and nurtured, as profitability became a greater issue for banks across the spectrum; thus has it become the latest bandwagon to join. Income from fees and commissions may be derived from a number of sources, including the selling of insurance or savings products; Allfinanz and Bancassurance are areas in which banks attempt to harvest this potential crop.

Joint ventures have been a common method for banks looking to manufacture their own insurance products. Insurance companies in their turn have been keen to enter such agreements as equal partners as it allows them to access the attractive distribution channels provided by bank branches. Examples of this approach may be found across Europe and are continuing: NatWest's accord with Clerical Medical has led to the setting up of Nat-West Life in the UK. In Spain, Banesto and the French insurance giant AGF have established a joint venture named Banesto Seguros to sell insurance through the branch network. Citibank's Bancassurance operation in Germany has been very successful, with products sold through its 300 retail branches.

Across Western Europe there is a trend away from simple low interest deposit accounts towards investment vehicles promising higher returns, for example life insurance, mutual funds and other country-specific products such as PEPs in the UK and OPCVMs in France. It is largely as a result of this trend that banks have entered the insurance market, and developed substitute products to protect themselves from the likely exodus of ordinary depositors.

Savings banks clearly deal with a clientele far less wealthy than that of private banks, and yet the lower rankings of HINWIs may well use their services. This is particularly true of the elderly, who may have many years of banking with such an operation, and individuals of wealth who are unsophisticated in expectation, or lacking in knowledge, as far as managing their investments are concerned.

At the same time, the growth in insurers' offerings in the investment market can also be seen to be eroding the available client list for the private bank.

The linkage between savings banks and insurers has much potential, and thus presents a new competitive area for the private bank at the lower end of the market. As already discussed, private banks are no longer able to count on managing the total wealth of their client.

The prevalence and role of savings banks varies from country to country within Europe. In the UK, there is only the TSB; in Germany, there are some 750 regional savings banks, with an aggregate number of 19,480 branches, and in France the 31 savings banks act as a single organisation. Italy's 83 savings banks are essentially autonomous. The function of savings banks has evolved quite radically in some countries, in recent years. Caja de Madrid and La Caixa, Spain's two largest savings banks, intend to develop into commercial banks with a national branch presence; Dutch savings bank Verenigdte Spaarbanken has changed its name to VSB Groep, and intentionally, its image.

Raising additional capital has been an issue for some savings banks, but in Germany these institutions have arranged for the provision of issuing shares without voting rights and dividend bearing bonds. The Swedish savings bank network has completed its merger plan with a national holding company, and complex reform has taken place in Italy, leading to cross-holdings between savings banks.

It seems that many European savings banks are set to extend their operations into fields other than straightforward retail banking, which of course includes insurance products. Thus the move from savings to wealth, through the route of insurance investment products, may be another chink in the private banks' armour.

NOTES

1 GAM Guide and Description.
2 Charles Handy, *The Age of Unreason*, 1989, London: Century Hutchinson.
3 Lafferty Publications, July 1992.
4 Paper given at the IBC 'Success in Private Banking' Conference, March 1993.

8

SECURITY AND COMPLIANCE

THE PROBLEMS OF WEALTH: SOURCES OF 'FUNNY MONEY'

For those of us without large fortunes for investment and management, there may appear to be no problems attached to managing wealth. When considering the security and legality of wealth investment, however, things are not as straightforward as they seem.

In 1991 British police and customs seized half a ton of heroin, a ton of cocaine and 31 tons of cannabis. The availability of heroin and cocaine has increased more than tenfold in the past ten years. It is generally estimated that seizures account for 10–15 per cent of available drugs. By noting street prices and allowing for reduced purity levels we can estimate that street level trafficking in Britain for these three types of illicit drugs alone could have generated more than £2.5 billion in 1991. These estimates are produced by calculations based on user/consumption and production assessment models. Whatever the true figure, beyond the obvious cost to the economy, there is also the cost of acquisitive crime committed to fund addiction, together with the costs of enforcement, lost production in industry, treatment and rehabilitation of offenders, and prevention.

The Group of Seven Financial Action Task Force estimates that between 50 per cent and 70 per cent of the proceeds of trafficking are available for laundering. The existence of London as a major financial centre also exposes its investment markets to abuse by those who launder the proceeds of trafficking generated in other countries. It is now recognised that money laundering is the most sophisticated element of organised criminal activity.

EMPLOYEE OFFENCES: THEFT AND FRAUD

Any bank is potentially at risk of and liable for employee theft or fraud. Opportunities and temptations should not, but probably do, increase with the available wealth being handled; certainly potential losses are much greater in the private banking environment.

101

Client relationship officers enjoy a powerful position in the direction and management of their client funds. This is particularly the case where elderly clients are involved, or a 'hold all mail' mandate has been authorised. Clients who prefer to pick up or review financial mail when making infrequent visits to their bank are often particularly concerned about confidentiality in their affairs: they have no wish to advertise a relationship with any financial institution, particularly foreign ones. Although banks do not encourage these accounts – they are expensive to administer – quite a high proportion of customers use this approach. With a lack of regular contact, and no forwarding of transaction details, this kind of account can present a particular risk, as was the case with a US private banker in 1990. She used an internal 'pending transaction account' device, claiming to have received telephone authorisation from octogenarian clients in Latin America to embezzle a total of $3.7 million over a period of 18 months. Serving a long prison sentence upon the woman, the US judge was particularly critical regarding controls in her unit.

The fraud only surfaced because the private banker used a company cheque to settle an outstanding credit card bill for $28,000. Her account was in dispute and so being watched over by the card company; if that had not been the case the payment irregularity could well have gone unnoticed.

The woman had become a close friend of another client, and used transfers from accounts which were not particularly active to bolster his funds. She also paid for travel, medical expenses and gifts for her family by the same route. In making his judgement, the judge expressed astonishment at the laxity of controls, describing them as 'non-existent or inattentive with respect to a situation so fraught with dangers of theft'. Little respect had been paid to bank requirements for written confirmation of transaction authorities; that others in her unit, including her supervisor, were happy to accept transfers of large sums on reported telephone conversations seems astonishing. Nor was the private banker's responsibility negligible; she handled the accounts of some 100 clients, whose funds totalled $275–80 million. More than 20 of these clients had 'hold all mail' accounts.

The position of trust in which a client relationship officer is placed of course runs in two directions: trust between client and banker, and trust within the bank. Control procedures and compliance must take this somewhat ambiguous situation into account, as the incident described above illustrates.

CROSS-BORDER SCOPE FOR MULTINATIONAL FRAUD

The necessity for international funds transfer, certainly a key element in the private bankers' armoury, creates further criminal opportunity. Although few cases are reported, great publicity is given to occasions where electronic funds transfers have been diverted for employee gain. External criminal activity is of course another problem in this area, with computer 'hacking' presenting a challenge – and potentially a highly profitable one – to the criminal computer boffin.

However, the main concern for authorities and banks alike is the preponderance of 'hot' money which can be channelled through legitimate operations. Quantities of cash, produced in relatively low denominations, through a variety of crimes and misappropriations, needs to be consolidated into a form of wealth more easily transported – especially out of jurisdiction. High turnover and low investment enterprises can be used to facilitate such a process: a number of the 'new businesses' in the cities of Central and Eastern Europe, for example, are restaurants with no diners, or stores with no buyers. An imperative for the money mover is avoidance of the creation of any external record, audit trail or paper trail leading to subsequent stages.

When the money has been converted into a transferable form, it will often be moved offshore. This places the funds beyond the reach of the legal authorities in the jurisdiction where the initial activity occurred. Even if the relevant laws are capable of application on an extra-territorial basis, and very few are, by involving another jurisdiction significant practical barriers are placed in the path of investigators in obtaining and securing evidence which would be admissible by a court. Certain jurisdictions are willing to offer banking and other facilities on the basis that secrecy will be assured; there are also countries which have been prepared to facilitate the receipt of money no matter what its source.

Once the money has been taken offshore it can then enter the conventional banking system, either directly or indirectly, and move through usual channels. It is clear that the amount of criminal effort and expense that will be required for laundering, for example, the profits of a major drugs operation, are rather more than would be required for frustrating a regulatory authority, such as the Taiwan Securities and Exchange Commission investigating insider dealing. Laundering operations will range from the most simple manipulation of accounts to structures involving hundreds of companies, with thousands of bank accounts. The larger the organisation that is employed to launder the money, however, the greater the costs and the higher the risk of detection or of something going wrong.

Recent investigations into hot money movement have identified individuals who have been prepared to service the financial interests of terrorists in Northern Ireland, bank robbers in England, drug dealers in Miami and fraudsters in Hong Kong, through the same offshore bank in the Caribbean. Many of these individuals are experts in financial and corporate matters and have created a network of corporate and other entities in jurisdictions not known for their willingness or ability to promote financial integrity. In a number of investigations they have been shown to be willing to facilitate other dubious financial and commercial transactions, in particular, to use their corporate entities and offshore banking facilities to front or give credibility to those engaged in advance fee frauds and the like. The modern money launderer is unlikely to be involved as a member of a criminal organisation, but much more likely to be on the periphery of the financial services or banking industry, or a professional adviser, such as a lawyer or accountant, who is prepared to make his services available to whoever is willing to pay.

IMPLICATIONS FOR THE PRIVATE BANKER

For European private bankers, the implications of money laundering, hot money and funds transfer are becoming much more important. Where before, as already stated, the principle of 'know thy customer' has been well subscribed, from 1 April 1994 in the UK, and soon after in other European Community Member Countries, this tenet will be more firmly enshrined within the law.

The European Directive on Money Laundering places an obligation on Member States to require financial and credit institutions and their directors and employees to cooperate with the authorities by informing them, on their own initiative, of any fact which might be an indication of money laundering. They must also provide all necessary information on request. The Directive also, except in relatively narrow situations, forbids a financial institution from further participating in a transaction if it suspects it is part of a money laundering operation, until it has made such a report. The UK's 1993 Act has created a new offence which has the effect that any person who, acting in the course of any trade, business or profession, knows or suspects that another person is engaged in money laundering shall be guilty of an offence unless he discloses to the relevant authorities facts that he knows or suspects as soon as is practicable. There are also of course questions of manipulation of flight capital, or the secretion of funds regarded by various government bodies as due to them.

There has been considerable discussion as to the requisite state of knowledge. The cases have indicated two basic standards, one requiring subjective knowledge, and the other a rather more objective or constructive standard. It was thought that the distinction could be justified in terms of whether the third party who facilitates the breach of trust comes into possession of the relevant property, or simply facilitates its control or retention by another. In the first case, a more objective standard was considered appropriate, and knowledge of facts which would put a reasonable man on notice that something dishonest was afoot would be sufficient to justify trustee liability. On the other hand, where the participation of the third party does not extend possession of the property, it was thought that the requisite degree of scienter should be actual knowledge. In view of recent cases, it seems that the question of knowledge is bound up with the nature of liability being imposed. Where the third party does not come into possession of the trust property or its proceeds, then it is difficult to conceive of them as a constructive trustee. The liability of such a person for participating in the breach of trust will be personal.

Although cases do indicate varying qualities of knowledge, it would seem the better view today that before a third party can be held liable as a facilitator it will have to be shown that he or she knew the facts or deliberately turned a blind eye and acted with a lack of probity. Thus, the prospect that a banker or financial intermediary could be personally liable for negligently participating in money laundering operations appears to be receding. However, the position is still not certain, and the courts are plainly unsympathetic to those who become involved in such operations. In a recent case, it was observed that the defendants 'made no enquiries . . . because they thought it was none of their business. That is not honest behaviour. The sooner that those who provide the services of nominee companies for the purpose of enabling their clients to keep their activities secret realise, the better.'

It is clear that the more information banking officials are required to obtain and test, the more onerous will be their responsibilities not only in regard to compliance with civil law, but also in regard to their duties under criminal law. The more that a banker is bound to know about a client the greater will be the obligation, for example, in the context of financial services law, to ensure that all financial advice is not only carefully given and researched, but is suitable to the circumstances of that particular client. By the same token, the more information is required according to due diligence and compliance procedures, the more difficult it will be for the banker to resist allegations that its involvement in a breach of trust was known, or at best turned a blind eye to.

Bankers, intermediaries and professional advisors are thus placed on the horns of a dilemma. They are being pressurised from a variety of irresistible sources to create more information, which will fix them with greater knowledge on the one side and yet, on the other, they are being required to assume responsibility for the integrity of transactions on the basis that they had knowledge, or should have had knowledge, of the relevant facts. It might not even be sufficient for an intermediary to deliberately curtail its access to information, as within both the risk of liability in the criminal and civil law, and certainly at the level of administrative and disciplinary proceedings, the requisite standards as to what information should be obtained and digested are set objectively.

The private banker is clearly in a potentially vulnerable position, given that the very nature of private banking is driven by the need for confidentiality and the 'regulatory-efficient' management of investments and movement of funds. One American banking operation is already taking the unusual step of having each and every potential new client checked out by a search agency before accepting them. Nor is the position clear in terms of international law, as was made clear in a recent case involving a trust company. The trust was set up at the behest of an individual who appeared to be the beneficial owner of funds and investments to be placed within the trust. However this was not the case, and the trust managers were alarmed to receive papers from a US court seeking reparation of $138m said to be part of the Marcos fortune. The sum involved was considerably larger than that managed by the trust, but because of US legislation the court was able to aggregate, and reach a huge figure. It is thus clear that due diligence investigations cannot be restricted to the merely obvious.

BURDENS OF COMPLIANCE

The new legal requirements create a burden of compliance, and a real set of pitfalls for employees in the financial sector. In the UK, non-disclosure of suspicion or information can attract a punishment of up to five years' imprisonment.

The major obligation is for all employees to report their knowledge or suspicions *either* to a police official *or* to a person in authority appointed for the purpose – the compliance officer, for example. This means that employers must exert a considerable degree of careful interpretation and sympathetic implementation when they create their internal reporting procedures. Young and inexperienced employees may find considerable difficulty in knowing how best to comply with these requirements, because of the legal expectation that staff will 'inform' on others, a cultural concept towards which many people will exhibit great personal antipathy. In addition, a compliance officer who does not act upon receipt of employee information is himself considered to have committed an offence.

The UK implementation of the Directive is very full: it has been calculated that there are 216 different ways in which it is theoretically possible to commit an offence under the new legislation. Ensuring that compliance procedures are clear, unequivocal and sufficiently flexible to enable staff to comply with the law is a considerable burden. Given that private banking staff are normally dealing with confidential transactions, frequently of considerable value, and with a high degree of autonomy and responsibility, the new requirements cannot be taken lightly.

Protection from unnecessary risk requires action on two fronts: continued and increasing knowledge of the client and his affairs, and wide-ranging policies of diligence, supported by extensive training. Diligence must start with an acceptance of the real meaning of the 'know your client' provisions, and the refusal to accept potential customers without determining their true identities, and having as detailed a knowledge as possible of business needs. Such provisions must be supported and assisted by good record-keeping and extended audit facilities.

In addition, there is an increasing need to 'know your introducer'.

Providing detailed staff training in the understanding of the sources of dirty money – a requirement backed up by the education requirements of the UK regulations – will provide staff with the extra degree of professionalism required to assist them in recognising and dealing with potentially dangerous transactions.

There are considerable dangers in adopting a relaxed attitude to the Directive and the resulting legislation. It is of course in the interests of any organisation to go beyond mere compliance with the law and develop a positive approach to combating money laundering. All individuals and organisations have a social responsibility to help control drug trafficking and organised crime, and enormous damage will be caused to the reputation of any institution which becomes associated in the public mind with laundering. This holds true even when such involvement is entirely innocent and is likely to be reflected in a serious loss of customer confidence, which, as has already been discussed, is a major selling point of the private banking institution.

Regulators will expect compliance with the new legislation. Those who fail to respond in an appropriate manner run the risk of losing their authorisation to operate in their existing markets. This concern should be considered at a domestic level and also be seen against the background of the international exchange of information by regulators when starting up a new operation overseas.

Even when an institution is used as an innocent vehicle for laundering, associated legal costs can be considerable if a case is investigated. Law enforcement agencies will seek to recover documentation, freeze accounts and finally recover the tainted funds. Lengthy legal disputes may arise if, for example, a client's company account is found to contain a mixture of illicit and legitimate funds.

TRADITIONS OF SECRECY

The requirements of 'due diligence' are of course intended as protection for the banks, as a means of identifying funds of doubtful origin. In countries where banking secrecy is legally cushioned, e.g. Switzerland and Luxembourg, the opening of a new account is a potential danger point – a difficult situation in an increasingly competitive market. The EC Directive on Money Laundering is legally not applicable in Switzerland as Swiss voters rejected membership of the European Economic Area in their referendum.

Swiss law does now insist upon the establishment of beneficial ownership. Individuals can no longer hide behind a lawyer or other professional advisor via the so-called 'super banking secrecy' of Form B. Thus the quality of an account's owner must be fully investigated before banks take on the risk of servicing it.

Unfortunately that was not apparently always the case: a letter circulated around Swiss banks and authorities a few years ago from a bank employee suggested that his employer had regularly turned a blind eye to the origin of funds – but since neither the employee nor the bank concerned was identified, verification of the claim was not made. The official line is that of the Due Diligence Agreement between the Swiss Bankers Association and the Swiss banks, which came into force on 1 October 1992. The agreement is a private one among all Swiss banks, established under the leadership of the SBA, and specifies that the banks contract to:

- verify the identity of their contracting partners;
- obtain from the contracting partner in cases of doubt a declaration setting forth the identity of the beneficial owners of assets deposited with the bank;
- and not to provide active assistance in the flight of capital and tax evasion.

The latter requirement is very specific, and of course has particular relevance to the Swiss private banker, or to private banks of other origination with operations in Switzerland. Banks 'may not provide any active assistance whatsoever in transferring capital outside countries whose laws prohibit said transfers or impose restrictions on the placing of funds abroad'. The definition of active assistance in some ways directly reflects the *modus operandi* of the private banker: it is not permissible to receive clients abroad by appointment outside the bank's own premises, for the purpose of accepting funds; nor to participate abroad in the setting up of offset transactions if the offset is aimed at furthering the flight of capital. Further, collaboration with third party individuals and companies may be suspicious, especially in cases where the bank is keeping their accounts.

BANKING SECRECY WITHIN THE EC DIRECTIVE: THE CASE OF LUXEMBOURG

Walking along the tightrope of maintaining secrecy within an EC framework is something that the Grand Duchy of Luxembourg has managed very well, and to some competitive advantage for its many banks. According to the laws of the country, any professional – including those in the realm of medicine – is bound to secrecy under penalty of a prison sentence. Thus at the same time as there is an obligation to bear witness, under EC requirements, there is no obligation to reveal: the banker has a choice.

With the advent of Article 41 (1), banking secrecy can be found in black and white in Luxembourg's legislation, and has been redefined, made more precise and strongly reinforced. However Article 40 requires professionals of the financial sector to declare on their own initiative to the Luxembourg public prosecutor's office any pertinent facts – solely to do with the suspicion of money laundering from the trafficking of drugs. Thus the principle of secrecy remains current, and Luxembourg bankers are hard put to take into account laundering operations other than those issuing from the most serious offences and crimes.

The importance of the coexistence of banking secrecy and a strong code of ethics is well understood in the Duchy, although other countries have accused the state of enabling a financial market whose primary activity would be to provide a privileged location for those wishing to launder funds. The official response is that as long as Luxembourg banks are able to remain faithful to their natural role as confidants to their clients, and not forced to assume a role as supervisors in the service of the EC, they will continue to bring committed and active support to their legal authorities in the fight against crime.

EUROPEAN DIRECTIVES AND THEIR IMPLICATIONS FOR PRIVATE BANKS

There are a number of key Directives that have either been adopted by the Council of Ministers or are under active discussion. The main Directives outlined here are:

- Investment Services Directive;
- Second Banking Directive;
- Capital Adequacy Directive;
- Insider Dealing Directive;
- Money Laundering Directive.

Investment Services Directive

The Investment Services Directive aims to establish a basis on which investment firms that are authorised in one Member State can provide investment services throughout the Community without further author-isation.

The European Commission is therefore attempting to set minimum standards which must be met by an investment firm in order to receive authorisation. It has been agreed that firms must have sufficient initial capital and that the directors themselves must be of 'sufficiently good repute and experience'. Any persons holding 10 per cent or more of capital or voting rights or exercising significant influence in the firm must be deemed 'suitable' for the task.

These items are necessarily vague because of the difficulties of establishing a consensus on precise capital limits and other guidelines. A separate Directive for Capital Adequacy covering both credit institutions such as banks and investment firms is being considered by the Commission and is outlined below. However, on the strength of the home country's authorisation, the Directive is designed to set out under what terms an investment firm authorised in one Member State can provide investment services into or establish a branch within another Member State. The development of this 'single passport' mirrors the work done on the Second Banking Directive, outlined below. Those institutions authorised to do investment business under the Second Banking Directive do not require authorisation under the Investment Service Directive. The majority of business rules remain a matter for the host state.

For the private banker, this has implications, and opportunities, for cross-border investment management. The Directive also includes provisions for compensation schemes, the exchange of confidential information between supervisory bodies and on relations with third countries.

Second Banking Directives

The Second Banking Directive permits credit institutions, such as building societies and banks, to carry out cross-border business within the EC without the need for further authorisation. The services covered by this Directive include securities trading, portfolio management and advice as well as deposit taking, lending, money transmission services, leasing and the issue of credit cards, all of which are of course highly relevant facets of private banking services.

The Directive sets minimum standards of authorisation and prudential supervision to be adopted throughout the Community including a minimum capital base of ECU 5 million for most credit institutions.

The Directive was adopted by the Commission in December 1989. The date of implementation for the Directive was 1 January 1993.

Capital Adequacy Directive

The Capital Adequacy Directive is still under discussion by the Commission but it aims to set minimum requirements for investment business activities of credit firms and institutions to be covered by the Second Banking Directive and the Investment Services Directive. Whilst the on-going capital requirements for most of a bank's business are set out in the Own Funds and Solvency Ratio Directives, it is possible that the investment business of a credit institution will be subject to the provisions of the Capital Adequacy Directive. This will, however, be at the discretion of the Member States. Most private banking operations are off-balance-sheet, but the amount of bank capital invested in this area will have an adverse effect on the capital ratio for other banking business.

The Directive sets out the level of initial capital required for investment firms and provides capital requirements to cover specific market risks.

Insider Dealing Directive

The Directive on Insider Dealing was issued in November 1989 and required all Member States to make insider dealing unlawful. The Directive also tied EC countries to cooperate in obtaining and exchanging information on insider dealing in order to promote the enforcement of the Directive.

The aim of the Directive has been to prohibit the dealing in securities by those in possession of price-sensitive information. In addition, the Directive prohibits the passing on of inside information as well as the recommendation to others to deal in securities on the basis of such information. The Directive also aims to clarify the position of market makers and analysts. Whilst this is not more important to private banking than to other capital market operations, it is clearly impactful. This is particularly true in terms of the 'Chinese Walls' which must exist between institutional business in a private bank, and private bank clients.

Money Laundering Directive

The Directive was created to ensure that 'prudential rules keep pace with the creation of the single European market in financial services' (Sir Leon Brittan on introducing the Directive in 1990).

The Directive itself states that 'when credit and financial institutions are used to launder proceeds from criminal activities . . . the soundness and stability of the institution concerned and confidence in the financial system as a whole could be seriously jeopardised, thereby losing the trust of the public'. The impact of this directive is discussed above. What follows is a more complete description of the requirements.

Organisations affected by the Directive

Credit institutions

Defined by reference to the first and second Banking Coordination Directives as any institution whose business is to receive deposits or other repayable funds from the public and to grant credits for its own account. This will include UK branches of non-UK institutions.

Financial institutions

These are defined by the Directive itself as being any undertaking other than a credit institution whose principal activity is:

- lending;
- financial leasing;

111

- money transmission services;
- issuing and administering means of payment (e.g. credit cards, travellers' cheques and bankers' drafts);
- trading for own account or for account of customers in:

  - money market instruments (cheques, bills, CDs, etc.);
  - foreign exchange;
  - financial future and options;
  - exchange and interest rate instruments;
  - transferable securities.

- participation in share issues and the provision of services related to such issues;
- advice to undertakings on capital structure, industrial strategy and related questions; advice and services relating to mergers and the purchase of undertakings;
- money broking;
- portfolio management and advice;
- safekeeping and administration of securities.

The life insurance activities of those companies and friendly societies subject to the provisions of the EC Life Insurance Directive are also covered.

Other

The Directive allows for the regulations to be extended to cover categories thought to be particularly susceptible to money laundering such as:

- accountants;
- auctioneers;
- casinos;
- commodity and commodity futures brokers and dealers;
- solicitors;
- licensed conveyancers;
- independent qualified conveyancers and authorised practitioners.

In the UK, HM Treasury has decided for the moment not to include these groups in the legislation, preferring to explore:

> how they might regulate their own activities to ensure that they do not leave themselves open to be used for money laundering purposes. If such self-regulation proves inadequate, we will need to bring forward further Regulations to cover a wide range of undertakings, in order to comply with Article 12 of the Directive.

9

DILEMMAS

The changes taking place in the European private banking market are significant, and offer both opportunity and challenge for the players. As has been shown, the market is huge, growing and looks very profitable – an attractive banking segment. However competition is growing – the 'me too' factor – and the need for differentiation is increasing as clients grow more sophisticated in their performance expectations, and yet demand the same or better levels of service. Specialist private banks will see more competition from the retail giants who have cottoned on to the potential profits; retail banks will find it difficult to change their culture from volume transactions to high value service.

A number of dilemmas face the private banks in their quest for even greater success, and are discussed in this chapter. They are:

- client profitability;
- differentiation in the market;
- exceeding performance expectations in service delivery;
- getting the product and service mix right;
- improving time-to-market;
- disintermediation
- riding the cash flow;
- human resources and rewards strategy;
- measurement.

CLIENT PROFITABILITY

The level of client activity is the key to client profitability. Those clients willing to 'churn' their portfolios – to actively manage and adjust for the best possible returns – are obviously the most profitable, generating transaction charges and commissions as well as management fees. It is also the case that a better margin is likely to result from clients with a portfolio of lesser value, in terms of management fee. According to Datamonitor's 1992 survey,[1] a UK private client fund manager can expect to achieve a 25 per

113

cent return on the commission deals that they instigate. The largest share is realised through the £250,000 to £500,000 portfolios. Taking into account management fees, commissions and additional administrative and other dealing charges, Datamonitor estimated that the total income from funds under management of £3.44bn was £35.8m. Of this, 65 per cent derived from fee income, with a further 16.19 per cent from administration services such as nominees.

Table 9.1 Client distribution by portfolio size, 1992

Net portfolio distribution	% Clients	No. of clients (actual)
Less than £100,000	5.0	400
£100,000–£250,000	21.0	1,680
£250,000–£500,000	59.0	4,720
£500,000–£1,000,000	10.0	800
£1,000,000–£10,000,000	5.0	400
Total	100.0	8,000

Source: Datamonitor, 1992

Table 9.2 Client distribution by value of portfolio, 1992

Net portfolio distribution	Average value holdings (£k)	Total value (£m)	% Value
Less than £100,000	85	34	1.0
£100,000–£250,000	200	336	9.8
£250,000–£500,000	340	1,605	46.6
£500,000–£1,000,000	680	707	20.5
£1,000,000–£10,000,000	1,900	760	22.1
Total		3,442	100.0

Source: Datamonitor, 1992

Table 9.3 Management income and commission charges, 1

Net portfolio distribution	Average management fee	Fee income (£)	% Value share
Less than £100,000	1.10	374,000	1.06
£100,000–£250,000	1.00	3,360,000	14.4
£250,000–£500,000	0.80	12,838,400	55.1
£500,000–£1,000,000	0.75	5,304,000	22.8
£1,000,000–£10,000,000	0.65	1,404,000	6.0
Total		23,280,400	100.0

Source: Datamonitor, 1992

Table 9.4 Management income and commission charges, 2

Net portfolio distribution	Average portfolio churn	Average commission rates
Less than £100,000	0.85	1.27
£100,000–£250,000	1.10	0.79
£250,000–£500,000	1.25	0.58
£500,000–£1,000,000	1.25	0.55
£1,000,000–£10,000,000	1.30	0.45

Source: Datamonitor, 1992

Table 9.5 Total client commission for the industry, by portfolio size, 1992

Net portfolio distribution	Average commission income	Total commission income	Commission average holding (%)
Less than £100,000	918	367,030	1.08
£100,000–£250,000	1,738	2,919,840	0.87
£250,000–£500,000	2,465	11,634,800	0.73
£500,000–£1,000,000	4,675	4,862,000	0.69
£1,000,000–£10,000,000	7,898	1,263,600	0.59
Total		21,047,270	

Source: Datamonitor, 1992

Table 9.6 Total client commission per fund manager, by portfolio size, 1992

Net portfolio distribution	Total commission income	% Share of commission income
Less than £100,000	91,758	1.74
£100,000–£250,000	729,960	13.87
£250,000–£500,000	2,908,700	55.28
£500,000–£1,000,000	1,215,500	23.10
£1,000,000–£10,000,000	315,900	6.00
Total	5,261,818	100.00

Source: Datamonitor, 1992

Table 9.7 Additional client fees, 1992

	Average additional charges	Total additional income
Less than £100,000	170	68,000
£100,000–£250,000	400	672,000
£250,000–£500,000	680	3,209,600
£500,000–£1,000,000	1,360	1,414,400
£1,000,000–£10,000,000	2,700	432,000
Total		5,796,000

Source: Datamonitor, 1992

Table 9.8 Total income by source, 1992

Activity	Total income (£)	% Value
Fee income	23,280,400	65.02
Commissions	5,261,818	14.70
Admin, e.g. Nominee	5,796,000	16.19
Other, e.g. Advice	1,467,360	4.10
Total	35,805,578	100.00

Source: Datamonitor, 1992

Most private banks are able to return around 50 per cent on capital invested, and see the line of business as a very lucrative one. Undoubtedly, the global players have an advantage in that their infrastructure is necessary and available for all activities, not just private banking. However the differentiation and identity of such divisions within a large universal bank can cause problems, both internally and in client perception.

Senior bankers expect rationalisation among their number. Coutts International's Michael Burmester sees problems ahead for banks who are unable to make the investments in IT, or who are not attractive as employers to top professionals; Georges Vergnion, at Chase, agrees and expects fewer but larger competitors as acquisitions provide the route to increased market share.

DIFFERENTIATION IN THE MARKET

The lack of differentiation between private banks is an interesting factor. Most players are offering very similar services to the same groups of clients and potential clients. Level of service and charges do not vary tremendously, and many institutions have similar approaches to stock selection and asset allocation. Although investment performance is likely to vary, with some banks managing to achieve significant leadership, the level of client knowledge and experience is, broadly, limited. First-time clients have little to go on in terms of rankings or performance indications: gaining a client, as in all sales situations, but much more obviously so in this sector, will rely on the level of rapport and trust achieved between banker and client.

Until now, this has not been a gating factor. An extremely high percentage of all new business comes via referral from existing clients and professional relationships, and with the expected growth in the market it would seem that private bankers do not have to worry unduly about differentiation from competitors. Established clients, however, will move their business if they perceive that service levels are not to the level expected or required. In addition, the greater knowledge and sophistication of upcoming private clients – those likely to inherit, who perhaps already have

MBAs – may well drive private banking business down a less profitable, more product-driven and therefore commoditised route. It is in those circumstances, as is apparent in the case of North American private banks, that differentiation becomes crucial.

Competition is perceived to be significant in these proportions: products, 29 per cent; services, 31 per cent; price, 32 per cent; convenience 7 per cent.[2] Banks who are able to evaluate their positioning and strategy in the light of these trends will maintain an edge by focusing on areas where they can maintain or improve their current position. The smaller traditional private banks are ahead of the game in their understanding of service, and their move towards institutional business as a means of sharing skills and infrastructure.

EXCEEDING PERFORMANCE EXPECTATIONS IN SERVICE DELIVERY

Private bankers, as one would expect, are well aware of the problems facing them in the industry over the next five years. Performance management is a key issue: with greater competition comes the need for superb performance. Many new clients come from the Asia Pacific region, an area where growth is 'like Topsy' and they have an expectation of growing their fortunes in the same way.

Continuity in relationships, an issue not solely confined to Switzerland, is also important, and despite the Swiss emphasis on training and expertise there still seems to be a dearth of talent in portfolio management in the country.

Creativity, in a risk-prudent culture, is a trait that will need nurturing, as will a degree of personal risk in intra-bank relationships. Whilst proper controls must of course be maintained, the command and control culture is an invalid one for the development and maintenance of a service ethos.

Swiss private bankers, with their history and experience, their ability to engineer high performance products, and their recognition of the importance of human relations, have a cultural edge. Competition will force this issue.

GETTING THE PRODUCT AND SERVICE MIX RIGHT

That products are important cannot be denied; that every private bank has a similar set is an unfortunate fact of life. However it is in the service delivery of those products that an edge can be sought and achieved, as the more successful private banks have long recognised. Key products for the moment are portfolio management, in-house funds and deposits; loans, foreign exchange cash management and trust are not seen as particularly important.

Demand is expected to increase for discretionary portfolios over the next five years, and given the level of regular and repeat fee income that can be attained, it is likely that trust business will be the next highly marketed focus area.

The most important factor affecting the client base is the provision of service, and many banks are seeing a need to realign their organisation to support this. Quality of service depends on expertise, procedures and systems, and superb customer knowledge: all of these tools can help build client relationships to a highly profitable level.

IMPROVING TIME-TO-MARKET

In analysing trends and forecasting the future for the private banking sector, it is all too easy to see no major changes: a growing market, reliance on service, continued product development, and a very healthy business to be in. But private banking, despite its roots in security and stability, is no less vulnerable to tremendous change than other sectors. Can the style of business bend enough to provide flexibility when necessary? To use the literary analogy, form must support content, and time-based competition will become increasingly important.

Product introduction may provide a two- or three-month advantage, but a competitor will soon have a copy-cat or better product on the scene; some development activity may take so long that the lifetime of the product is much reduced, and therefore its cost is prohibitive. As HSBC's Richard Moseley points out, banks and clients are climbing up the same learning curve, but banks must be ahead. Packaging what the client needs, and doing so quickly before interest is lost, provides a crucial difference between success and failure in the client relationship.

Many US banks bemoan their lack of ability to spot re-engineering opportunities: improving time-to-market has become a critical area in which this technique can be profitably used.

DISINTERMEDIATION: A THREAT TO PRIVATE BANKING?

As communications and techniques improved in the 1980s, the greatest threat to the banking community as a whole was disintermediation: the ability of large companies to organise their own financial transactions without the need of intervening and costly banks. The threat continues, demonstrated by banks' own efforts to continue to control payment networks, share settlements, and the growing use of electronic data interchange (EDI) developments.

Undoubtedly, private banking provides a service for the wealthy and the busy: those whose concern is for maintenance and enhancement of their lifestyle and power, but who do not have time or interest to invest in managing their investments. Citibank and ANZ-Grindlays have identified increasing instances where financial intermediaries are expanding their influence – because HINWIs are looking for dedicated advice.

The communications boom makes it possible, even easy, for intermediaries to step into the world of private banking. Information is widely available; what counts is being able to interpret the information and turn it to advantage. Bankers, the original intermediary between investor and industry, may find themselves having to worry about being mediated against. Perhaps that is why ex-investment bankers for the American houses are becoming the new disintermediaries.

In the USA, there is a difference between the *wealthy* client and the *successful* one (who of course is also wealthy). The difference is in the use of credit. The successful client, more sophisticated, with greater expectations, and a fuller awareness of financial services and markets, is likely to want to use lines of credit as much as make time deposits. This is a much less profitable business, and, of course, a riskier one for the banks themselves. Private banking services in Europe do not include lending as a matter of course, and even then, only on a fully secured basis. Demographic changes, however, suggest that the 'baby boomers' generation will have an effect in this area. Whatever the age range, it is increasingly likely that HINWIs will engage financial advisors to manage their affairs with banks: a wedge in the traditional relationship. The growth in specialism itself suggests that a new career track could be emerging with the growth of individuals with access to wealth. If that is the case, the private banking operation may find itself relegated to the role of transaction organiser and fund manager, no longer holding the pivotal relationship, nor its leveraged fee income.

RIDING THE CASH FLOW

Capital flow, as has been pointed out by more than one senior banker, is the infrastructural underpinning of continued success. Capturing clients' cash flow will determine the quality of the business, and of course will require international presence in order to manage its many dimensions and directions. Yet greater reliance will need to be placed on information technology, with associated expense. Communication, now crucial between bank officers and clients, will become even more important within the banks; integration, long a dream, will become essential. Functional integration will require private banks to look at their business processes very carefully, and adopt techniques which allow them to improve cycle times – for product development, marketing activity and settlement.

One-dimensional flow of capital will be a thing of the past: while bankers may talk about managing a level of client assets in a particular location, it is likely that the client funds will be managed *from* a location rather than *in* a location. Associated with the flexibility of funds location will be a greater degree of risk, which must be addressed. The larger banks are already well down this road, but smaller organisations, who perhaps use another bank's infrastructure to transfer funds around the world, will need to pay this significant attention.

HUMAN RESOURCES AND REWARDS STRATEGY

Organisationally, banks will find themselves considering a balance between reputation, innovation and integration. Reputation will drive the need for skills, but these may become more generalist than specialist: outsourcing of non-core work will mean that specialism can be bought when it is required.

Private banking is a knowledge business. The knowledge required is of the client, the professional banking environment, and ways in which to facilitate action. Management skills will focus far more on teamwork, and team measurement.

Human resource management will assume a new importance, as staff see less career progression but require tangible and intangible rewards: the trend for churning key staff may become as pronounced as in the heady days of London's Big Bang – and that would be extremely deleterious for the private bank.

MEASUREMENT

Like their American counterparts, private banks in Europe will find it essential that they can accurately measure the cost of managing, maintaining and acquiring relationships. Another scenario may see wealth management moving downstream, to the well paid rather than well breeched. If that is the case, transaction costs will become even more important, and price-sensitivity will grow. Undoubtedly, the emergence of private banking as a good business to be in – which of course it always was – will influence the banking sector as a whole. It would be nice to think that the greatest influence will be on customer care; if service becomes a differentiator both ends of the spectrum will have to differentiate their service.

Marketing will become increasingly important: it simply will have to happen. Private banking is currently experiencing the first level of growth shared by IT companies: everyone wanted the power and advantage technology could bring, just as more private clients want more and better service and performance. The market is already becoming fragmented, and may move to saturation within ten years as every provider of banking services decides that a piece of the action is for them.

The dilemma being produced by larger banks' arrival and concentration on the scene is one of polarisation: the high and low ends of the market.

While the 'high perceived value' of private banking has more attraction than the 'low cost transaction' of the retail market, providers must move both higher in perception, and lower in activity cost in order to maintain competitive advantage.

CONCLUSION: CHOICE IS EVERYTHING

The single most important factor in the future shape of private banking is choice: the client's choice of bank, of relationship, and the professional's choice of employer. The private banker of the future could be a reinvention of his ancestors: a friend, advisor, counsellor and entrepreneur. The challenge for banking organisations is to allow such an anomaly to exist.

NOTES

1 Datamonitor, Private Banking and Client Services, May 1992.
2 Price Waterhouse survey, 1993.

10

WHAT THE BANKERS SAY

In researching this publication, a series of interviews with key figures in private banking provided much information. The interviews ranged over a variety of topics: from the market and its future potential to the skills and investments needed; from emerging areas of interest to product development. What follows is a selection of comments and opinion from leading private bankers.

ON THE MARKET

It's profitable, growing, and will be much bigger by 2000.

Warwick Newbury, Coutts & Co.

Just to jump in now to get 3 per cent up-front commission for a particular product and be cash rich for an enterprise is very short term, and you are out of the market the next year or the year after.

Werner Peyer, Crédit Suisse

In the Middle East, the heyday of high turnover, highly speculative days has gone. The Middle Eastern client is not an easy target now, he has good advisors (many who used to work for US banks), which was not the case ten years ago. It's much more of a casino.

Andrew Wimble, ANZ Grindlays

The typical client at Pictet would be in the range of SFr1m upward, but we do have a lot of clients who have less, obviously a lot who have more. We'd never put that up as a limit in any way. Obviously everybody knows that small clients who have been small clients for ages suddenly become very large, they sell their business, or they inherit. It's more the relation and the quality of the people with whom we build those relations that we look for rather than the immediate minimum profitable size of the account.

Ivan Pictet, Pictet & Cie

The competition in France is strong, it is a well-served market . . . not from the very large wealth, that has always been international . . . the smaller and medium-sized wealth that has not traditionally been very internationally-minded, and is becoming more so . . . which gives us the opportunity on the international investment side and the treasury side.

John Goodwin, Citibank

Worldwide, private banking is a big market measured by revenue stream – £15bn is an estimate of overall revenues available worldwide. There is still a big revenue in standard products and insurances; private banking is in its infancy as far as the profit potential is concerned. Research shows that the barrier to private banking growth is people thinking that the service is not for them.

Warwick Newbury, Coutts & Co.

The private banking market will grow by itself, people are producing wealth . . . we have to remain attractive; to identify where the greater potential areas are for us . . . be attractive, find the ways to get known to this segment of the market, which is developing . . . but there is no one formula for that.

Ivan Pictet, Pictet & Cie

It is true that the new generations are more ready to take some risks, and if you look at what is going on in Latin America with Mexico recovering and Venezuela and Asia fast growing, a lot of our clients are interested in investing there. Sometimes they don't know about those areas, but they want to test it because there is an interest. So what we do is, because of our knowledge of that part of the world, we are able to set up for them what we think are good investments and put them there.

Georges Vergnion, Chase Manhattan

The interesting thing about private banking is that there is no marketing to be done. The marketing of private banking is done through the institutional side and through the existing network of clients, but otherwise it's extremely difficult. You don't knock at the door of a wealthy individual and tell him you'd love to manage his money, that would be a very awkward approach, so in fact there is no typical marketing approach for private banking.

Ivan Pictet, Pictet & Cie

WHAT PRIVATE BANKING IS ABOUT

The essential is that we go out towards the client, that we get out of our offices, either physically or by the phone, we accompany the client truly and intervene at any possible moment in his lifecycle to be there as a partner. And that we show interest in having him as a client. That is essential, that to me is the activeness or pro-activeness. Then if we are there with him and we understand his need, we are there with the right service or product. Then the client also integrates us in his thinking for the future.

Werner Peyer, Crédit Suisse

We are still not the bank of the sort of new rich aggressive entrepreneur. We are perceived as the bank which is looking for a long-lasting relation and which will not provide the sort of short-term performance orientation which some people in a hurry would be tempted to look for.

Ivan Pictet, Pictet & Cie

This activity as far as we are concerned is an evolving activity which requires more talent, expertise and investment on a solid foundation built by others. There are some good newcomers of quality and some fashions which will disappear in the future. There might be some changes in terms of minimum size . . . somewhat below what we feel is the line of what clients will require in the future, and what firms will be able to invest in technology, etc. . . . a line below which it would be hard to offer that full-fledged activity.

Thierry Lombard, Lombard, Odier & Cie

Because he is a businessman and he travels, we accompany him basically with our network on his journeys throughout the world; we offer him services particularly on an overall global picture of his assets, we offer a service of consolidating these assets on a computer simulation, we approach him with all his different needs, so that he has a partner for all his financial needs. So we're not focusing purely and do not just show interest in buying and selling stocks and bonds or running a current account. That's what we also call a private banking approach *à la* Crédit Suisse.

Werner Peyer, Crédit Suisse

We are a global bank. Wherever the client feels comfortable and sees an opportunity, we'll be there to serve them.

Georges Vergnion, Chase Manhattan

ON ATTRACTING CLIENTS

On the client acquisition side we have noticed it again and again . . . and on the recruiting side . . . it's always the name. . . . About two weeks ago someone was sitting there from a good competitor . . . who said, 'Basically I'm quite happy where I am and I don't really want to change but if I change I want to change to the top houses, and for me one of the top houses is UBS.' . . . So it makes it easy then. The name is one thing, the other thing is the network we have worldwide, the representative offices, the fact that we have been in the market for 128 years.

Peter Braunwalder, UBS, London

Referral is a tradition we particularly value as a way of measuring our clients' satisfaction . . . it is a positive *a priori* and awareness *ex ante* of what we can offer. Second is curiosity . . . looking at the markets and the world in general to establish where there could be a need for a specialty. . . . We are constantly abreast of new developments in the markets and also of course the competition . . . and the third is linked to the very nature of the clientele which is more easily identified if we talk about institutional clients . . . one of our means, or vectors to bring these clients to us . . . is to know where they are and to have the right product at the right time . . . to be there and go actively and to present ourselves whether through trips or maybe through presentations.

Patrick Odier, Lombard, Odier & Cie

Clients want to talk to experts. . . . We are doing all of that better, doing a better job reaching the clients locally in the countries and then bringing them the capabilities we have locally in these centres as well as in the investment centre.

John Goodwin, Citibank

We must not hide that we have also taken profit from the political decisions of our neighbours. One which had a very important influence was the introduction of withholding tax on capital revenue in Germany, so it's not only the effort and the innovation which brought the money to Luxembourg, but also the decisions of the people abroad.

Lucien Theal, ABBL, Luxembourg

What we have done now, developing over the last year or 18 months I suppose, is a concept called country market management, and through analysing the client base we've got, and the potential of various countries, which means going through political data, economic, market analysis, market research, etc. We've now identified something like 15 countries, or in some cases groups of countries around the world . . . where we believe the potential is and where we should be looking for new clients. Each of those countries has allocated to it a country market manager who in addition has got his own group of clients who he is looking after, and that country market manager is totally responsible for all marketing activity that Coutts International is doing in those countries.

Michael Burmester, Coutts International

There is, of course, a difference between institutional client marketing and private client marketing, and they are totally different in many areas. The HINWI does not want to be attacked by sales people, he does not want to be offered every day for breakfast, lunch and dinner . . . when you have reached a certain level of confidence with a client, therefore, the introduction to potential new clients is of extreme importance and we do encourage our client officers to *dare asking*. This is a change in our marketing approach. Traditionally Swiss bankers did not dare to ask questions.

Werner Peyer, Crédit Suisse

You need personnel who can identify themselves with the firm and who can also understand what kind of clients we are looking for . . . there is no concession to quality, because . . . the cost of acquisition is extremely high in this business, and therefore we are interested to create a long-lasting relation.

Ivan Pictet, Pictet & Cie

ON CLIENT NEEDS

Continuity is an important factor for the client. Through the years . . . one of the things that helps us is being eight managing the firm; it gives us first the capacity to know the clients from many sources, to know their satisfaction, to be quite early in feeling if things are not going quite well for that client.

Thierry Lombard, Lombard, Odier & Cie

There is always a trade-off between volatility and liquidity and return . . . if you can start to blend that more effectively you will continue to develop really good relationships with these clients. Some of the product capability will be increasingly important for us and to make sure that we leverage the franchises as the business evolves. . . . To maintain that strong relationship overlay with a degree of continuity. . . . We have to develop relationship managers in that regard, and develop the clients, and make sure that nothing moves too slowly or too fast.

Richard Moseley, HSBC

There are more and more new private clients who want to have private client services as offered in Switzerland, but nearer his home, in the most convenient place. He has not the same needs any more as the traditional private client, he does not seek banking secrecy . . . but is more concerned about performance, accessibility, a wide range of products and maybe with discretion rather than secrecy.

Werner Peyer, Crédit Suisse

Certainly today's client, with the competitors around, is very critical of fees as well, and he compares then the services offered with the fees paid. If the ratio's right, and the performance, and he is at ease with the institution, and he can relate to the ethics of the bank, then he is likely to be staying with the bank and is going to be a very loyal and a very interesting client. Interesting not only in the term of profitability, but in being involved with the bank, using the bank as partner in different aspects, and that's private banking for us.

Werner Peyer, Crédit Suisse

ON THE PRIVATE BANKING ENVIRONMENT

I don't think we should say that it was all solid and safe in the old days and now it's more entrepreneurial. There were some shades of black and white going on and probably still are – but less so because of due diligence, compliance, better MIS . . . it's no longer possible to run these kinds of portfolio without management being fully aware of the make-up and the risks being taken, and quite rightly so.

Michael Burmester, Coutts International

We must keep a good balance between the two activities. If one slows down then the other will keep the financial centre going. Then we must think, do we have to find new niches . . . and in the field of financial engineering there is still a lot to do . . . on the side of private banking you must not change the activity but you must improve it.

Lucien Theal, ABBL, Luxembourg

Banks and clients are . . . both climbing up the same curve and we have to be ahead. In the Middle East this is particularly so, UK clients always have been quite sophisticated, and there are new wheezes coming along . . . clients are interested in some investment in real estate and they want a cap in the rates, for example . . . but how do you package it, how do you make it happen very quickly?

Richard Moseley, HSBC

Some banking analysts would say that in terms of quality earnings, in particular because fee income is repeatable, £1 of private banking fee is probably equivalent to £2 of more volatile earnings. Private banking has a lower risk profile.

Warwick Newbury, Coutts & Co.

COMPETITION IN PRIVATE BANKING

There is no growth in this market in Europe. The only way to grow is to take market share. So we are being aggressive in our marketing: we are hiring people, good quality people, we are training them a lot, we are providing products that they need very quickly, we are investing in technology, and so on, so that's the way we do it. Altogether they make us very attractive.

Georges Vergnion, Chase Manhattan

We still have room! We are happily developing our *fonds commerce*, what is important to us is to see that for private clients and institutions around the world there are more or less 10–20 names potentially where you know that you would be getting . . . value in investment and good service and what we want to be there is on that list . . . during the past year there are 3–5

Swiss names, of which we are one, and the European level again and the international level again.

Thierry Lombard, Lombard, Odier & Cie

This is not a high capital business – with the exception of lending, which is only one of many private banking services.

Warwick Newbury, Coutts & Co.

There's a perception, isn't there, that private banking is a good area to be in, and because one of the main areas is experience and customer advisors who have been in the game a long time and have got the contacts, it isn't one of the things that you can just plunge into overnight.

Michael Burmester, Coutts International

There is no Machiavellianism about the Swiss, they are extremely straight-forward. So in a certain way banking in Switzerland has lacked a little bit of imagination, you might say, if you compare it with Anglo-Saxon banking. But it has gained strength which of course means that out of ten banks with triple A ratings there are three Swiss, the three biggest Swiss banks . . . Pic-tet has a triple A, from Bankwatch on IBCA, which has given us the highest mark too.

Ivan Pictet, Pictet & Cie

Technology certainly can give a competitive edge. Private banking is an information business, client information is key.

Warwick Newbury, Coutts & Co.

It's a big strength that we have as part of a large group: we have a lot more *potential* to make things happen, and the competitive edge is that we have the *ability* to make it happen. So to bring in the expert where appropriate, to make sure we've identified sufficiently the needs of the client, that we hand-hold him and make sure with the product provider that we deliver the goods.

Richard Moseley, HSBC

I would think the US banks in general are much more advanced than the rest of the world, than the European, Japanese, any other banks, you will not see that cultural diversity elsewhere and . . . Chase is certainly well ahead in that.

Georges Vergnion, Chase Manhattan

Coutts cost:income ratio is 68. That's good, but some people are aiming at 50. This is a people-intensive business. Relationship management and good people are expensive.

Warwick Newbury, Coutts & Co.

The Big Three [Swiss banks] will go down a little, they need to shape up to face a very strong and stiff competition, and therefore they have major

cultural problems to go through . . . that will take them a long time. . . .
The Big Three will lose more than they attract . . . we will take more out of
them, the Swiss private banks will take more of it probably too. I think that
the foreign banks, the strong foreign banks (the weak ones have already
gone), we will have a good growth, and the good Swiss private banks will
have that as well. The financial intermediaries, the good ones, will expand
their influence, because people will look for dedicated advice. That's why
the Swiss private banks are successful, because that's what they
do . . . that's what I see as big trends.

René Boehrer, Citibank

Greed is our biggest competitor.

Ivan Pictet, Pictet & Cie

ON SWITZERLAND'S PLACE IN THE
INDUSTRY

What you are seeing in Switzerland is that 15 years ago you had about 30
Swiss private banks, 15 years later you have only maybe 15 left. So you are
seeing acquisition, to close the gap, between what we are and what they
used to be.

Georges Vergnion, Chase Manhattan

Our challenge is always to identify changes in time and to adapt to them in
time. We have as much feeling of the market. Switzerland has this challenge
of remaining Switzerland and keeping its attractiveness. That's not the
challenge of Pictet as a bank, but for all Swiss banks.

Ivan Pictet, Pictet & Cie

The question of Europe is one of many elements . . . Switzerland cannot make it without being in Europe, our wealth relies on 60 per cent
outside trade, a very important import/export trade, we rely on personnel
mobility.

Patrick Odier, Lombard, Odier & Cie

If you take what is the total private banking wealth in the world, and the
last figure I saw was $3 trillion or was it $4 trillion, about 50 per cent of that
wealth is managed in Switzerland. That's another interesting thing, it may
not actually be in Switzerland, it may be in London or New York, but it's
actually managed from here . . . there can be little doubt that Switzerland is
still the number one country when you are looking at a league ranking, or
league table.

Michael Burmester, Coutts International

Europe should not remain a foreign entity to us for too long.

Patrick Odier, Lombard, Odier & Cie

The emphasis is away from Switzerland being a safe haven . . . and coming far more to a performance-driven ethic . . . it's another reflection of . . . the border lines becoming very blurred.

Michael Burmester, Coutts International

It is quite difficult for us to work out the true effect of the Swiss vote not to join the EEA. If anything we probably gained more business. Although the proposed agreement did not cover things like banking confidentiality, I think some of our clients were more comfortable with Switzerland not being part of it. In this matter client perception was the important thing.

Georges Vergnion, Chase Manhattan

The Swiss environment had started changing much before that . . . Switzerland is in a much more open and compatible position, *vis-à-vis* the rest of the world, in comparison with what it has been in the past. . . . There are still obstacles remaining that are negative, and that have pushed us to do things we couldn't do outside.

Patrick Odier, Lombard, Odier & Cie

We are going beyond the London–Switzerland dimension, which is already too small for our clients and us . . . we tended to have a professional from London go and sell Switzerland and vice versa . . . it is a common standard that we handle clients of the US or South America over here and the account and the money remains in the US, and the trading relationship remains where the centre of expertise is . . . the old booking centre is *dépassé*.

René Boehrer, Citibank

The challenge for Swiss banking is on the one hand changes that may not occur from support by politicians. Private banking has always depended very strongly on favourable political conditions. That was the myth of private banking within the confidential/secure environment. This is not going to change. We will have a different political environment for the future. . . . We have perhaps lived in isolation . . . now we are becoming more involved . . . thinking about joining the EEC. . . . This might have an impact short term on our clients, certainly our traditional private clients. Our politicians will have an impact on how they treat the banks in taxation. . . . On the other side, the challenge is how these many, multitude of operators will behave in their ethics. If private banking as such is not dented by certain people who are just out to make commissions and therefore damage the overall reputation. The third one is that these new players do not become pure stock pickers . . . being capable of offering a variety of services . . . and responding to market changes, personal changes, to environment changes. To shape up their reputation for this overall global approach.

Werner Peyer, Crédit Suisse

THE FUTURE OF PRIVATE BANKING

Keeping standards as high as they can be is our biggest challenge.

Ivan Pictet, Pictet & Cie

I think the environment ahead of us with a positive GATT outcome and the single market is very positive, people will be exporting more, going outside more, and they will need advice, they'll need opinions . . . so then they can decide what they want to do.

Rene Boehrer, Citibank

A lot of people talk about quality service . . . not quite so many people manage to deliver . . . to use the overworked phrase value-added, what the support services sector can bring into the whole equation is to deliver that first quality service and to get it right first time.

Michael Burmester, Coutts International

We see trends in terms of newcomers, people not devoting enough patience, structure, investment and expertise in succeeding with their services, . . . also fashion in some cases. There is short-term motivation in trying to grab or benefit from one activity whereas you need to be more patient, make more effort and more investment to succeed. That trend has been there for quite some time, and there are waves of newcomers disappearing, coming back, changing for the time being. What is interesting is that five years ago there was not much media interest in private banking.

Thierry Lombard, Lombard, Odier & Cie

You are going to see less competitors, but those who remain are going to be bigger, like us, because of the cost of acquisition, the cost of relationships, we are going to see that a lot. It will continue in fact. We are going to see a need for resources, money, a lot of money, technology, being global, people investment, training and so on. I think in Europe you are going to see people looking for market share and I am certain you are going to see niche players, which are small banks in their own particular niche, you know, with their own particular geography. I think they will survive for a while. But you are going to see more competitors, maybe not from the banking environment.

Georges Vergnion, Chase Manhattan

There will be a strong demand for good services, good performance, and a good future for that activity.

Thierry Lombard, Lombard, Odier & Cie

TRENDS FOR THE FUTURE

The capital flow moves much faster than it used to, and so people want to take advantage of the opportunities around the globe. That's why it's very important to be a global organisation.

Georges Vergnion, Chase Manhattan

131

I think like in other forms of banking there's going to be some form of rationalisation. I think there are going to be some smaller players who can't afford the investment necessary in IT, who won't necessarily be attractive employers for the top professionals in the market, who won't be able to afford the product development, in other words who won't be able to keep up with the huge investment that's going to take place.

Michael Burmester, Coutts International

Our challenge is the impact of the potentially low interest rate environment. That is the catalyst for people looking at alternative forms of investment which will generate a higher rate of return. When interest rates were high, there was very little catalyst for doing things – with interest rates where they are, there's much more of a catalyst. I think that means the people who are going to be successful are those who are going to give some increased earnings potential without a significant increase of the volatility in the underlying asset value. That's something which we've worked on, looked at some product for the larger clients, we can do that through derivatives, etc.

Richard Moseley, HSBS

One trend that's obvious is sophistication, client sophistication, around the world . . . we're doing things around the world which a couple of years ago we would not have dreamed of . . . but one other interesting trend that seems to be happening is this whole dynamic between onshore/offshore. A few years ago . . . people said the money is going back to onshore countries . . . with the repatriation of funds to Central America, in Europe with the single market, and we could talk about other regions of the world. One of the interesting things is you will not see this one-dimensional flow. I think the reality is that we are going to have risk around the world, and that will be one reason why we will continue to see money going back and forth, and of course that's one reason why places like London do well.

John Goodwin, Citibank

Crédit Suisse has had a long-standing tradition in private banking, it was established in 1856, our private banking activity is over 100 years old, and therefore you could assume that the old money is an essential part. The only problem is that you don't want to rest on what you have acquired, but you want to continue and develop, and you don't want to get an image that focuses only on one segment. You want to be looking into the future and to be recognised as a bank that looks into the future and therefore the focus on new money is essential.

Werner Peyer, Crédit Suisse

AMBITIONS FOR THE FUTURE

Going forward our strategy is to be astride those [cash] flows. If you want to be a full-service private bank, you have to be talking to the client in his country if he is willing to do wealth management business there . . . and you also have to be in the key investment centre.

John Goodwin, Citibank

We don't want to grow or develop ourselves beyond what we think is any reasonable size, which we think is what we have in terms of quality of people . . . we are happy as we are for the time being . . . developments have been good over the last ten years in terms of new clients and new markets.

Thierry Lombard, Lombard, Odier & Cie

In the field of private banking I think that we will improve our situation as a centre, as a leading centre, of investment funds . . . I think we will not create a new activity but improve that activity towards the private client, but on the other hand we will have more innovation in the field of financial engineering, and this is geared more towards companies and institutions.

Lucien Theal, ABBL, Luxembourg

THE INFRASTRUCTURE CANNOT BE IGNORED

You need good MIS, and I think one thing we do have here, although it's by no means perfect, we do have very good MIS here. We are able to cost out per client, per product, the cost of delivering.

Michael Burmester, Coutts International

Many banking skills, ranging from the basic, but incredibly important money transmission, our ability to get money from here around the world is a key factor.

Richard Moseley, HSBC

GROWING THROUGH CLIENT REQUIREMENTS

The newer clientele . . . has another advantage for us which is the development of newer competencies . . . because of the precision of needs these clients have brought us a range of new competencies whether through hiring people or developing these specialisms, which today, and hopefully tomorrow, we will more and more apply to the rest of our clientele.

A historical example is the development of our fixed income competence . . . which really started with our efforts towards institutions which we established through our London presence some 25 years ago, and has now developed I think into one of the recognised leading teams in managing international fixed income portfolios.

A second example could be the hedging techniques in the field of ForeX, where we have also been asked to develop a more sophisticated approach to

ForeX globally . . . including the mastering of new instruments . . . but rather than looking at those instruments as representing sources of primary profit in the trading aspects . . . they incorporated new techniques to manage the more complex environment of foreign currencies.

Patrick Odier, Lombard, Odier & Cie

We are looking more at derivatives and emerging country markets and we'll need to take a slightly different view because with the US so low on dollars, they're more tempted to look at alternative investments. . . . It's all about making sure that you help clients get in at the right time, and that's an investment issue all over the world.

We don't want to find that we're getting new business and losing old clients. They've got to be bedded down, be satisfied.

Richard Moseley, HSBC

That is one of the essential marketing approaches, asking clients and then involving clients much more in the bank's operation, so that he is comfortable coming here, and there is not a certain fear of stepping into the palaces of a banking institution. Very often we have with new clients what we call in German *stellen-angst*, the fear of 'stepping over'. In all the banking and marketing strategies that you see everywhere, it's the friendly bank. Well, we want to be friendly, competent and efficient, make the client at ease and involve him in the banking process that is related to his account. We often had the traditional image of the banking patriarch sitting behind his desk, and it was the client who had to ask for service. Today of course we act as partners to the client.

Werner Peyer, Crédit Suisse

WHAT MAKES THE DIFFERENCE?

If you can sell the Swiss strength with a little touch of Anglo-Saxon sophistication you've got the best product that is available.

Ivan Pictet, Pictet & Cie

Performance – product performance is more and more important as clients become more sophisticated. That's where the winners will win and the losers will lose.

Warwick Newbury, Coutts & Co.

It's a core competence required by the client that we can offer . . . augmented by the product skills offered by the group. . . . The relationship manager is obviously the *entrée* to the services of the group which the normal individual client would not be able to access very easily . . . and to mobilise the group's strength for a smallish client as opposed to the corporate client.

Richard Moseley, HSBC

The Chase name is a name which opens the doors, then you have to have the professionals, who have been properly trained to deal with clients. You need to have the sort of professionals who are able not only to identify but also anticipate clients' needs before they recommend a particular solution.

Of course, clients' business and professional interests are increasingly interlinked. Say clients are in an exporting business, than as a private bank we also need to find solutions to help them to export. We can do this because Chase has the range of corporate services to support the traditional private banking products. If we can help those private clients who have a wide range of business needs, then we are really adding value and they, in turn, will be likely to refer us to friends.

Georges Vergnion, Chase Manhattan

I think that when you look at products and services, or whatever you care to call them, one bank is more or less like another. One bank might have a three-month lead at one time, and another time someone else has a two-month lead but it's the service and delivery that's going to differentiate one bank from another.

Michael Burmester, Coutts International

BANKING CANNOT EXIST IN A VACUUM

One always has the possibility to block a law . . . there is always something in the law that displeases people . . . so the government is obliged to go through this somewhat painful consultation process so that there is no blockage to the law . . . it also has the drawback that we can't move very quickly on the legislative field.

Michel Derobert, Groupement des Banques Privées

Tax legislation would have an impact if the Inland Revenue was to make London a less attractive centre. . . . The UK has to encourage it, be keen to encourage foreigners to come to the country, acknowledging that although they have certain tax breaks they also spend a lot of money, and bring a power to the economy which is important, so it's more of a political, UK issue. Also in the UK, London retaining its strength as an investment centre . . . expertise still remains in London.

Richard Moseley, HSBC

ALL THE FINANCIAL CENTRES HAVE
ADVANTAGES

London is the most international financial centre in the world. New York is a domestic market, Tokyo is a domestic market, Zurich is probably the most international after London. We have a presence in all of them.

Peter Braunwalder, UBS, London

You will continue to have places like Switzerland and London as centres of expertise.

René Boehrer, Citibank

London appears slightly more sophisticated, although from what I have seen I do not think London has more sophisticated products. I think London is more product-oriented, and Switzerland is more service-oriented, but Switzerland is now becoming more product-oriented.

Ivan Pictet, Pictet & Cie

LUXEMBOURG'S PLACE IN PRIVATE BANKING

One must not forget that the financial centre [in Luxembourg] is first a private banking centre for the people living around the country. It is only on the second base you have people from South America, Eastern Europe, coming to invest. This is linked to the characters of the investors, who want to know their banker, speak to them and get advice. It is a question of confidence and in that sense it's a little bit difficult to get people from thousands of miles away. The main clientele comes from the area . . . Europe . . . to give you the whole figure . . . the northern part of Italy is now a new part of the area. The classical part is Germany, and then of course the Belgians, the traditional clients of Luxembourg banks for 70–80 years, because Luxembourg has monetary union with Belgium.

Lucien Theal, ABBL, Luxembourg

IT'S A PEOPLE BUSINESS

Our competitive advantage comes by having exceptional standards of ability, and measuring performance throughout.

Warwick Newbury, Coutts & Co.

The client is the bank's client and so the whole bank can help the client. There is a lot of teamwork, not only within private banking, but also within the corporation, so everyone is winning and everyone is being rewarded through this process.

Georges Vergnion, Chase Manhattan

The paramount challenge? Hanging on to the people, the good people that we have . . . we have a good strategy, we know what we want to do, we have an action plan, we have tested the strategy, we know what needs to be improved, what we need to work on . . . we are in execution mode, so therefore you need people, the good ones, and we need to hang on to them.

René Boehrer, Citibank

Pro-active is certainly the key word. My account officers ask me what is the difference between pro-active and active. I say if you've been passive up to now then active is good enough!

Werner Peyer, Crédit Suisse

The right quality relationship managers are crucial. It is absolutely prime because if that's not right other things don't happen . . . the core competency has to be relevant to the client.

Richard Moseley, HSBC

We are rewarding by results more – more for performance, an improved PRP. There is more emphasis on cross-selling. We now separate management of relationships from management of products, to ensure that all products are professionally managed.

Warwick Newbury, Coutts & Co.

The big banks usually in the good years in the 1980s had a turnover in Switzerland of 15 per cent of personnel, and the international banks . . . had a turnover of maybe 30 per cent. We have never had a turnover exceeding 3 per cent.

Ivan Pictet, Pictet & Cie

There are about 12 different nationalities working in the organisation, not only for language skills, but also for the culture. Each one of them does at least three weeks in training, product, management, a lot of money is being spent on training.

Georges Vergnion, Chase Manhattan

We develop staff to match the more sophisticated world in which they are working. Derivatives, options, control. Financial planning becomes more and more complex.

Warwick Newbury, Coutts & Co.

The Big Three Swiss banks are considered as the breeding ground for highly qualified account officers, who then are bought at a high price by those banks that do not have the training facilities as we do. Our apprentices at 16 already have the top apprenticeship for three years. People who graduate from university again get a special two-year course to turn them into bankers, so they are hunted regularly and we are faced with very stiff competition there on the labour market, because these banks do not invest themselves in the training, they simply increase the salary substantially.

Werner Peyer, Crédit Suisse

Becoming a partner is really like being married, you are giving all your strength and ability to the bank, and you can't afford not being totally comfortable with your partners.

Ivan Pictet, Pictet & Cie

ON CAREERS IN THE INDUSTRY

[Private banking and financial engineering] both have one necessity . . . the quality of the people working in the banks.

Lucien Theal, ABBL, Luxembourg

We always take juniors. It is very seldom that we take a full formed trained manager, we like to shape them ourselves and send them abroad and build this typical company culture.

Ivan Pictet, Pictet & Cie

We offer a door into a world of immensely diversified contacts and freedom of initiative, which . . . comes from the wealth of clientele. This is very motivating for young people, coming from a different horizon . . . because of the size which is quite modest, we try to keep a degree of flexibility and line of reporting which is as short as possible. There are no barriers for the younger people of our staff to bring their ideas to the attention of top management, and then be rewarded in terms of that good idea with a project being launched and getting the project.

Patrick Odier, Lombard, Odier & Cie

SECURITY, SCANDAL AND RISK

The security side has been a very strong factor and is probably still a main factor in the attraction of Switzerland. This might tend to erode because of the greater safety that one can see now in other countries. I think it's not Switzerland losing competitiveness, it's other countries gaining competitiveness in that sense, but the Swiss franc is not the only strong currency now. Switzerland is a very independent-minded country.

Ivan Pictet, Pictet & Cie

Reputational risk is a potential inhibitor. You need to be very cautious. There have to be many checks before opening a relationship.

Warwick Newbury, Coutts & Co.

I think unfortunately there'll be some players who'll get caught on bad risks and will have to call it a day anyway, and so I see a sort of concentrating and a narrowing in the market.

Michael Burmester, Coutts International

PRODUCTS AND THEIR LIFECYCLE

We have withdrawn the passbook! Products have an incredibly long life-cycle – they are being continuously improved.

Warwick Newbury, Coutts & Co.

We can bring new investment opportunities to the client . . . one of the interesting things particularly in view of the single market is an exposure management product where we will sit down with the client and review the client's balance sheet and talk about potential interest rate exposures or potential currency exposures. We then . . . put together a tailored proposal to deal with those risks . . . and over time stay in touch with the client and explain what has been dealt with.

René Boehrer, Citibank

We do not have a central unit that develops products for the job of developing products and throws them onto the markets and then we send our sales force out to sell products . . . it is not just a shot in the air where you launch a product and hope that a lot of people will subscribe to it, and then a year or two later you have to withdraw it again.

Werner Peyer, Crédit Suisse

ON EMERGING MARKETS

One element there is to make sure that we don't focus on an emerging market because it's fashionable . . . but only as an alternative, risk-controlled way of adding assets to our client's portfolio. We are keen on developing that awareness, of what is the development of the emerging markets, but not as an obligation because it's a fashion, to ensure that we are there if risk-wise it adds performance.

Patrick Odier, Lombard, Odier & Cie

In Singapore and Hong Kong, even in Taiwan over the last 20 years, it is incredible to see today what has been built, the level of disposable household incomes, and how it has been developed. Kuala Lumpur almost didn't exist . . . but there have been huge realisations there, very big fortunes made, very interesting people. They are usually very much based around the family, and this is something that is an asset for us of being Swiss. We base our image, our services, our products, on the knowhow based on tradition. Pictet has the family aspect, those countries and the people there can identify themselves quite well with what we are representing, so I think we have a slight advantage over the big banks which have a much more impersonal approach. Those families in these countries have groups or parts of their families spread out in the other regions and therefore when you touch one part you get more and more acquainted with the others.

Ivan Pictet, Pictet & Cie

ON CONFIDENTIALITY AND SECRECY

In Luxembourg we have a very sound protection of the private sphere in our legislation. Our authorities consider that the money you have earned is a part of your private sphere, and even the public authorities don't have the right to interfere in that private sphere so it's absolutely logical that you assure a bank's secrecy, and this will be not only the position of the present government but will last for a long time in Luxembourg.

Lucien Theal, ABBL, Luxembourg

The key point to understand about taxation is that Switzerland is a *safe* haven rather than a *tax* haven. Most clients choose Switzerland because of its solid reputation for security, stability and, of course, its private banking tradition. Those who are investing internationally are also often looking for products and services which are not available in their own countries. This is why, for example, many Middle Eastern clients who live in very low taxation economies choose to invest a share of their assets through Switzerland.

Georges Vergnion, Chase Manhattan

Scandal is always something that is possible in financial areas and if you have a big financial centre you probably have more risk to have a financial scandal than if you live in the middle of the woods. Usually the private bankers are extremely cautious and very prudent, and usually very old, so really it's not in their interest to take any sort of risk, especially as they are partnerships, so they traditionally do all they possibly can not to put their reputation at stake, because it's a long reputation that can be lost very quickly. Everything can happen but if you are very prudent, if you take less risks, if you know the people you are working with, these small entities are easier to look after.

Michel Derobert, Groupement des Banques Privées

The talents and the super performers, you can always buy them. To create a sophisticated product is not difficult. . . . More important is to keep one's reputation. A big bank will always get away with something. We have been here for 200 years now, and could lose everything in five minutes.

Ivan Pictet, Pictet & Cie

THE CLIENT VIEWPOINT?

They think we are top-notch! Look at the growth.

Georges Vergnion, Chase Manhattan

We should be where the client needs us to be. We are already largely there today . . . if anything we're putting our investment into building up our strength, in terms of product, relationship, management, technology in those investment centres, and then in the onshores doing the same thing.

John Goodwin, Citibank

It would be unthinkable for us to ask our clients why do you like us, in the institutional yes, but for private clients, this is totally adverse to private banking I would think. If people are your clients, the day they don't like you they will leave you.

Ivan Pictet, Pictet & Cie

THE LAST WORD

I wouldn't be surprised if like many other industries after the tremendous commoditisation and technologisation we go back to the essential: there is a human being who needs to see a human being, who wants to talk things over.

Patrick Odier, Lombard, Odier & Cie

APPENDIX 1

How the UK security systems work:
The Financial Intelligence Unit

Following the introduction of asset confiscation laws in 1987 a Financial Section was established with the National Drugs Intelligence Unit, with responsibilities in three main areas:

1 Financial intelligence;
2 International cooperation;
3 Liaison.

On 1 April 1992 the NDIU became the Drugs Division of the National Criminal Intelligence Service.

FINANCIAL INTELLIGENCE

The Drug Trafficking Offenses Act 1986 enables financial institutions to disclose suspicious money laundering activity to the authorities. Similar arrangements exist under the Criminal Justice (Scotland) Act 1987. In 1989 this facility was extended to cover other serious crimes and terrorism under the Criminal Justice Act 1988, and the Prevention of Terrorism Act 1989 (Part VI). With the agreement of law enforcement agencies and banking associations the NCIS Financial Unit acts as the national focal point for the dissemination of that information to operational police and customs officers.

Most United Kingdom organisations providing financial services have established internal systems whereby a suspicion generated at branch level is referred to a head office inspection department which is then responsible for making the report to the NCIS. The Financial Unit researches the information, before passing it on to the appropriate police force or HM Customs team, for investigation by a financially trained officer. The institution is protected by law in making the disclosure and is allowed to continue operating the customer account.

Increasing disclosures

Since 1987 the annual number of disclosures made to the NCIS has increased each year, to a figure of nearly 12,000 in 1992. About 70 per cent of disclosures are allocated to the police and 30 per cent to HM Customs. A small proportion initiate new investigations which result in the detection of crimes, the seizure of drugs and confiscation of assets. A further proportion are found to be significant in existing operations.

Details of financial investigations conducted by police and customs teams are recorded on the NCIS computer system. The Financial Unit is closely involved with the development of financial intelligence.

INTERNATIONAL COOPERATION

The Drug Trafficking Offenses Act also gives powers to courts to restrain and confiscate drug assets, in respect of both domestic and international cases. The UK has concluded a number of bilateral confiscation agreements with countries which have compatible confiscation or forfeiture laws and has designated those countries which have the 1988 United Nations Convention. In September 1992 the UK was the first country to ratify the Council of Europe Convention on Laundering, Search, Seizure and Confiscation of the Proceeds of Crime, which provides a multilateral framework for cooperation and reciprocity.

In conjunction with the UK Central Authority (the Home Office), the NCIS Financial Unit assists in the coordination of requests made under these confiscation agreements, and provides the means for assistance at the formal level whilst not interfering with informal, 'intelligence gathering' levels of liaison. The Unit also gives assistance to case officers involved in international investigations, through a range of contacts in overseas agencies.

LIAISON

Liaison is the third area of responsibility for the Financial Unit. It participates in working groups established by a range of domestic and international bodies with an interest in the study of money laundering. The Unit has assisted in a Home Office review of confiscation law; the G7 Financial Action Task Force; considered ways of providing guidance to banks and building societies on the subject of money laundering and facilitating their identification of suspicious activity. This resulted in the publication of Guidance Notes on Money Laundering for Banks and Building Societies, and later by Guidance Notes for Insurance, and Investment Businesses.

Investigation of drugs money laundering

All police forces in the UK have trained and designated financial investigators who work as specialists in asset tracing and money laundering cases.

In larger forces and regional crime squads these officers form specialist teams. HM Customs and Excise have specialist officers within the Drugs Financial Investigation Branch of the Customs Investigation Division. A survey of officers in May 1991 indicated that they are engaged in reactive (normally post-arrest work) for 80 per cent of available time, 15 per cent on pro-active, or targeting work, and 5 per cent on intelligence development. All officers who are involved in the investigation of money laundering and asset tracing attend a training course which conforms to a national standard.

It is considered good practice to assess the potential of a proposed operational target on a preliminary net-worth-income basis before operational resources are committed. Additionally the information from banks, accountants and others will indicate associations which otherwise might not be known. The information discovered by these means may be adduced during a trial, usually when it deals with evidence of inexplicably high expenditure. A financial component is therefore an essential element of any drugs investigation.

In cases involving crime other than drug trafficking, the Criminal Justice Act 1988 does not itself permit production orders, but orders for the production of documents and other material relevant to a criminal investigation can be obtained under the Police and Criminal Evidence Act 1984. There are some disadvantages in pro-active investigating in that these orders must relate to a complete offence.

Confiscation law

The Powers of Criminal Courts Act 1973 enables courts to order forfeiture of a defendant's property which was used or intended to be used in the commission of any offence. This power has not been widely used. The Misuse of Drugs Act 1971 gave courts the power to order the forfeiture of articles associated with the commission of drugs offences. This often involved the forfeiture of a drug dealer's cash and its award to the enforcing agency, but normally for only small amounts. These provisions, which remain in force, have been superseded by the introduction of new confiscation or forfeiture, and in this sense there are no civil forfeiture procedures for criminal offences. A second principle is that confiscation should be considered before any other financial penalty.

The United Kingdom introduced legislation to confiscate the proceeds of drug trafficking in January 1987. It is known as the Drug Trafficking Offenses Act 1986. For an investigator this legislation complements traditional drug investigations in several ways, including investigative powers, restraint and confiscation of drug-derived assets in domestic and international cases, together with a money laundering offence which provides an ability for any person to disclose suspicions to appropriate authorities with protection from breach of contractual confidentiality.

The Drug Trafficking Offenses Act 1986 was followed by the introduction of measures to tackle assets derived from other serious crime and terrorism in mid-1989. The Criminal Justice Act 1988 contains similar provisions for confiscation of assets derived from indictable crime. Whilst it does not create a money laundering offence, it allows voluntary disclosure of suspicion with protection from breach of confidentiality.

International cooperation

The Drug Trafficking Offenses Act 1986 acknowledges the international nature of drug trafficking and permits the investigation of drug-related assets held in the United Kingdom regardless of the locus of the offence from which they were derived. However these powers are restricted to evidence gathering in the UK, unless a Confiscation Agreement is in existence.

Such Confiscation Agreements under the Drug Trafficking Offenses Act or the Criminal Justice Act permit reciprocal investigation, restraint and enforcement of confiscation orders in respect of assets held in the United Kingdom where the originating offence occurs in another jurisdiction. These Confiscation Agreements are negotiated with jurisdictions which have compatible confiscation legislation.

The first Confiscation Agreement for the United Kingdom was with the United States and it came into force in April 1990. Several formal requests have been processed, but few forfeiture orders have yet been enforced. Under the Drug Trafficking Offenses Act (Designated Countries and Territories) Orders 1990 and 1991, agreements are also in force with Australia, Bahamas, Canada, Cayman Islands, Hong Kong, Mexico, Switzerland, Spain and Gibraltar. Further Confiscation Agreements have been concluded by the United Kingdom and are awaiting introduction in respect of the following countries: Anguilla, Argentina, Bahrain, Barbados, Bermuda, Germany, Guyana, Italy, Malaysia, Montserrat, Nigeria, Saudi Arabia, Sweden and Uruguay. A further 28 countries which have ratified the 1988 Vienna Convention have been designated by the United Kingdom. The Council of Europe Convention on Laundering, Search, Seizure and Confiscation of the Proceeds from Crime was ratified by the United Kingdom in September 1992 and will further widen the range of jurisdictions with which reciprocal forfeiture or confiscation can be carried out.

Money laundering

The Drug Trafficking Offenses Act created a money laundering offence, which is committed by any person who, knowing or suspecting that funds, property or investments are the proceeds of drug trafficking, assists another person to retain or control those funds. There are statutory defences to this offence, *inter alia*, that one did not know or suspect that the funds were the proceeds of drug trafficking; that one had disclosed, or intended to disclose, to a police constable the facts on which the suspicion was based. Any disclosure made under the Act will not constitute a breach of civil contract.

The police may consent to the continued operation of the account in circumstances which might otherwise amount to the commission of this offence. This allows the account to continue in operation whilst being investigated, despite the suspicion, and introduces the means for bankers to be protected when law enforcement agencies are aware of the true nature of a customer's activity.

The Criminal Justice (International Co-Operation) Act 1990 created a new offence of concealing or transferring the proceeds of drug trafficking and extends the offence of money laundering by creating an offence committed by a person who conceals or disguises the proceeds of his drug trafficking, or who converts or transfers that property or removes it from the jurisdiction, for the purpose of avoiding prosecution for a drug trafficking offence, or the making or enforcement of a confiscation order.

Identification of suspicion

The Bank of England as the supervisory authority for British banks has endorsed the provisions of the Basle Statement of Principles and requires banks to demonstrate their compliance with the statement. The Building Societies Commission issued to supervised societies a Prudential Note which also endorses the statement.

The British Bankers Association have funded the production of a training package for staff of banks and building societies which includes an introductory video, computer-based training and training for managers. This training system has been widely introduced since Autumn 1991.

APPENDIX 2

Money laundering pointers set out in 'Guidelines for the combating and prevention of money laundering' issued by the Swiss Bankers Association in June 1992

A customer's declarations regarding the background to such transactions must be checked for plausibility. Not every explanation offered by the customer can be accepted without scrutiny.

GENERAL POINTERS

The following transactions are associated with a notable risk of money laundering:

- transactions whose form suggests that they might be intended for an illegal purpose, or the economic purpose of which is not discernible, or which do not appear to make economic sense;
- transactions in which assets are withdrawn almost immediately after being deposited ('pass-through-accounts'), unless the customer's business activity furnishes a plausible reason for immediate withdrawal;
- transactions which cannot be reconciled with the usual activities or clientele of the bank or branch office in question and in which the customer's choice of that particular bank or branch office for the transaction cannot be ascertained;
- transactions which, in the absence of any plausible reason, result in the intensive use of what was previously a relatively inactive account;
- transactions which are incompatible with the bank's knowledge and experience of the customer in question or with the purpose of the business relationship.

Basically, it is justifiable to suspect any customer who furnishes the bank with false or misleading information or, without offering any plausible reason, refuses to provide information and documents required routinely by the bank for the business relationship.

INDIVIDUAL POINTERS

Counter transactions

- exchanging a large amount of small denomination banknotes (Swiss or foreign) for the same amount in large denomination notes;
- frequent changing of large amounts of money without using a customer account;
- withdrawing large amounts by means of cheques, including travellers' cheques;
- purchase or sale of large amounts of precious metals by an 'interim customer';[1]
- purchase of bank cheques on a large scale by an 'interim customer';
- transfer of money abroad by an 'interim customer' in the absence of any legitimate reason;
- repeated counter transactions just below the limit requiring identification of the customer.

Bank accounts and safekeeping accounts

- closing and opening new accounts under the same name or in the name of members of the customer's family without leaving any documented traces ('paper trail');
- frequent withdrawal of large cash amounts which do not appear to be justified by the customer's business activity;
- a customer relationship with a bank which does not appear to make economic sense (large number of accounts with the same bank, frequent transfers between different accounts, exaggeratedly high liquidity, etc.);
- provision, without any discernible plausible reason, of collateral (pledge of assets, guarantees) by third parties unknown to the bank who have no identifiable close relationship with the customer;
- transfer of money to another bank without indication of the beneficiary;
- payment orders with inaccurate information concerning the person placing the orders;
- repeated transfer of large amounts of money abroad accompanied by the instruction to pay the beneficiary in cash;
- large and frequent transfers from and to countries in which narcotics are produced;
- provision of bank guarantees or indemnities as collateral for a loan between third parties that is not in conformity with market conditions;
- cash payments remitted to a single account by a large number of different persons;
- requests by a customer that certain payments should not be effected through his account(s) but through the bank's nostro accounts or sundries accounts;

- unexpected repayment of an overdue credit without any plausible explanation;
- use of pseudonyms or numbered accounts for effecting commercial transactions by enterprises active in trade and industry.

Fiduciary business

- back-to-back loans without any identifiable, legally admissible purpose;
- holding in trust of shares in unlisted companies, the activities of which cannot be ascertained by the bank.

NOTE

1 An interim customer is one who is not a regular customer of the bank office in question (i.e. does not maintain an account or safekeeping account, safe-deposit box, etc.).

APPENDIX 3
EC Directives affecting private banking activities[1]

Legislative and fiscal regulations are becoming increasingly complex, and represent one of the major areas of concern for private bankers worldwide. EC harmonization decisions in the finance sector are far from simple to implement, and discussions and guidelines for practitioners abound – and are necessary. The following pages give an overview only of current issues and interpretation.

Solvency ratio

Council Directive of 18 December 1989 on a solvency ratio for credit institutions

This Directive establishes that the solvency ratio, i.e. the ratio between a bank's own funds and its assets weighted according to the level of risk, must be a minimum of 8 per cent.

Deposit-guarantee schemes

Commission Recommendation of 22 December 1986 concerning the introduction of deposit-guarantee schemes in the Community

Recommends that in all the Community countries, deposit-guarantee schemes should be established – i.e. schemes which provide, to a certain degree, for depositors to be compensated in the event of the bankruptcy of a credit institution. It likewise recommends that such schemes should also cover deposits held in branches of any bank with a head office located in a Member State (host country principle).

Collective investment funds

*Council Directive of 20 December 1985 on the coordination of
laws, regulations and administrative provisions relating to
undertakings for collective investment in transferable securities
(UCITS)*

This Directive allows a UCITS to market its units freely in all Member
States provided that it is duly approved and supervised by one Member
State and that it meets certain minimum requirements (structure, activities,
disclosure of information).

*Council Recommendation of 20 December 1985 concerning the
second sub-paragraph of Article 25 (1) of Directive 85/611/
EEC(85/612/EEC)*

Recommends to the component authorities of the Member States that if the
concept of 'significant influence' is represented in another Member State's
legislation by a numerical limit, they should ensure, if so requested by that
other Member State, that such limits are observed by investment and
management companies situated within their territory when they acquire
voting shares issued by a company established within the territory of a
Member State where such limits apply.

*Council Directive of 22 March 1988 amending, as regards the
investment policies of certain UCITS, Directive 85/611/EEC on
the coordination of laws, regulations and administrative
provisions relating to undertakings for collective investment in
transferable securities (UCITS)*

This Directive increases the maximum ceiling that a Member State can
impose with regard to the possibility of a UCITS investing its assets in
the securities of a single issuer (previously 10 per cent; now 25 per cent).

*Proposal for a Council Directive amending Directive
85/611/EEC on the coordination of laws, regulations and
administrative provisions relating to undertakings for
collective investment in transferable securities
(UCITS)*

Proposes to extend the single market for UCITS to money market funds
and funds of funds. Also permits funds covered by the proposed Directive
to invest in bank deposits. Extends choice of depository.

Capital adequacy

Council Directive 93/6/EEC of 15 March 1993 on the capital adequacy of investment firms and credit institutions

This Directive defines the rules on own funds of investment firms and the amount of their initial capital. It establishes the framework for supervision of market risks in general, and includes the investment activities of banks. Due for implementation on 31 December 1995.

VAT on gold

Proposal for a Council Directive supplementing the Common System of Value Added Tax and amending Directive 77/388/ EEC: special scheme for gold

This proposal provides for the exemption of 'investment gold' from VAT. Physical delivery of investment gold and gold 'other than investment gold' is subject to the normal VAT system.

Transparency of cross-border payments

Commission Recommendation of 14 February 1990 on the transparency of banking conditions relating to cross-border financial transactions

Recommends that institutions carrying out international transfers should ensure that their customers are properly informed on the 'price' of such transactions and that these are executed rapidly and correctly.

Money laundering

Council Directive of 10 June 1991 on prevention of the use of the financial system for the purpose of money laundering

Imposes certain obligations on financial institutions: identification of customers with whom they enter into business relationships; identification of customers carrying out transactions amounting to ECU 15,000 or more; conservation of certain documents. There is a requirement to notify suspicious transactions, involving in particular cooperation with the authorities and training of personnel, etc.

NOTE

1 *Source*: Banking Federation of the European Community.

APPENDIX 4
The players: who, where and what? Switzerland: Big Three versus tradition

Traditional Swiss private banks operate as partnerships, with each partner having unlimited liability for the bank's operations. Founded in much the same way as English merchant banks, numbers of private banks have declined over the last ten years. Well-known names such as Lombard, Odier and Pictet, the two biggest of the Genevois banks, continue to thrive, basing their business on the old values of service and relationship. The nature of the banks' structures means that little financial information is available about them; this is not required to be published under Swiss legislation, and the banks have been very wary of disclosing their positions.

Lombard, Odier

Founded in 1798, Lombard, Odier continues its traditional emphasis on asset management, but with growing awareness of the need to gain entrepreneurial clients as well as maintain relationships with wealthy families, the 'old money' of Europe. The bank compares itself to the major international banks as bespoke providers of wealth management services, rather than off-the-peg services. Services include brokerage, execution of securities trading, the sale and purchase of companies, direct investments and block trading, and tax and legal specialisation for estate planning and company and trust formation. The bank is present in most of the international finance centres: London, Amsterdam, Hong Kong and Tokyo, and has a seat on the New York Stock Exchange. Other offices are in Gibraltar, Jersey and more recently in Bermuda, with a specialist trust company.

Bank staff are young: the average age is 37, and of the eight partners, 49; partners on the board of management average 42. Members of the original Lombard and Odier families are key players, and the bank has invested heavily in information technology, a function managed by the youngest partner, Patrick Odier. The portfolio management system is said to be a 'dream machine'. Moves into institutional investment management have proved profitable in leveraging new individual business: as the bank had gained considerable expertise in managing the pension fund of their own employees, they began to market this new strength in the late 1960s, and now find some 40 per cent of assets managed are institutional. The small London office had management and advisory fee income of £4.4 million in 1992, against a total income of £4.7 million.

Pictet

Like Lombard, Odier, Pictet also operates as a partnership, and prides itself on the direct communication between partners and staff. Every day begins with a breakfast meeting between partners and portfolio managers to ensure that all issues and opportunities are known and discussed, followed by research meetings where analysts make their market recommendations; Pictet staff are encouraged to approach partners directly with proposals, and decision-making is very swift.

Pictet's assets under management are reckoned to be around $35 billion, although 1993 figures were probably nearer $40 billion. In 20 years, partner Ivan Pictet estimates that the bank's business has grown fivefold, with a staff increase of half that factor.

Institutional business is key to Pictet's growth, and some senior figures in the bank argue that private banking cannot exist without the institutional side: economics of scale are provided by common research and trading, especially the large-scale analysis of portfolio data, and both sectors support each other in finding and developing the new client base. The institutional side, largely driven out of the London office, is fast developing its Global Custody operation, and is seeing growth in its North American operation as well as in parts of Europe; it has been regularly listed within the top three on Micropal for emerging markets business. Approximately $300m in assets is managed from the London office, from some 600 clients.

In a survey of private bank charges in Switzerland, Pictet's fees were in the top half, and competitive with US levels – indeed, some US investors find the fee level surprising, at around 0.8 per cent for a globally mixed portfolio of bonds and equities to a threshold of $500k.

Pictet's human resources strategy values staff highly, with as much as two-thirds of their total compensation package in bonus payments; staff turnover is minimal, and long-term employment is the expectation rather than the exception. Like the other Swiss private banks, Pictet invests large amounts in staff training, through the Groupement des Banquiers Privées Genevois in Geneva, which has its own off-site training centre.

Results and directions for the Swiss Big Three banks are in some ways incomparable with the traditional, smaller players. However, it is clear that the profit levels of the small private banking operations are very

*attractive to the universaal banks of Switzerland, and of course to other
international banks.*

Swiss Bank Corporation.

SBC is the second largest of the Swiss 'Big Three', and continues its
expansion as a universal bank. Within that overall category, it moved into
Allfinanz in 1993, and strengthened its private banking and trust franchise
by forming a new private banking group in 1992. To do this, it combined
four old-established banks: Adler & Co., Bank Elinger & Co., Armand Von
Ernst & Co., and Ferrier, Lullin & Cie, which are wholly owned by SBSI
Holding AG – which vehicle is in turn 68.8 per cent owned by Swiss Bank
Corporation. Also part of SBSI is the Banca della Suizzera Italiana, which
became part of the group in 1992; ownership was consolidated in 1993.

Outside Switzerland, SBC's policy includes concentration on high net
worth individuals, with a view to offering integrated and customised products with high added value. The 1993 reorganisation into Domestic and
International and Finance Divisions allows the Domestic Division to segment customers and distribute products to them by grouping: sub-segments
are middle and large corporates and institutions, private investors and retail
customers.

SBC is the first major Swiss bank to create a Global Compliance focus,
with organisational structures in each major trading centre now being
developed and finalised.

Like other Swiss banks, SBC sees considerable opportunity in emerging
markets, particularly Latin America, and is strengthening trading activities
in the area. To gain access to the Mexican equity derivatives market, a
strategic alliance was formed with the Financiero Banamex-Accival (Banac-
ci) group. Similar partners have been found in South East Asia, with the
purchase of some 28 per cent of the capital of Public Consolidated Holdings Sdn. Bhd. in Kuala Lumpur, giving access to a seat on the Kuala
Lumpur Stock Exchange; in Thailand, a joint venture with Premier Finance
and Securities Company Ltd is intended to focus on the securities business,
corporate finance and fund management and research.

In 1993, SBC grew consolidated assets under management by 9.9 per
cent, and the number of investment customers' services by 3.2 per cent.
Approximately 25 per cent of the latter also hold securities accounts. Of the
total 2.2 billion customers, 91.6 per cent are private clients – which includes
all kinds of investors and savers. HINWIs constitute 6.5 per cent of the
client base, i.e. around 149,000, and are defined as having assets greater than
SFr300k, a relatively low threshold. The number of clients having assets of
considerably more than SFr300k is not available. Under the aegis of SBSI,
the private bank has managed to strengthen its market position for the bank
in Switzerland, growing assets by 9.2 per cent. The foreign branches and

subsidiaries of BSI and Ferrier, Lullin manage considerable assets, and Luxembourg and Monte Carlo subsidiaries, as well as branches in Hong Kong and Singapore, contributed to the growth of aggregate assets deposited as international units grew by 11.9 per cent.

The London operation sees benefit in combining the qualities of Swiss private banking with the very different skills available in the financial centre; there is a more aggressive approach to portfolio management in the UK, and the focus is on international, rather than domestic, clients. The style of delivery differs depending upon location, and must cater to the image that clients have of *either* the financial centre *or* of SBC. Not all clients value the same parts of the private bank, and with the increased sophistication and expectation of London-owned clients, there is a growing proportion who are influenced by the relationship between price and performance, rather than the management of the client–bank relationship. Trends foreseen include alternative investments to cash, and the use of complex instruments, in packaged forms, for example derivative products put together with a 'simple' explanation.

SBC attributes much of its success in portfolio management to flat-fee packages, which cover nearly all the bank charges involved. These have been popular with foreign private investors in Switzerland, with a 40 per cent take-up at the end of 1993.

In the trust business, the Grand Cayman operation attracted significant new business in 1993, while standard products did well in Nassau and Jersey. Realignment of North American and South East Asian organisations is expected to contribute to the expansion of the global private banking activities.

Table A4.1 Assets by customer category at the end of 1993: SBC Group

Private investors (assets > SFr300k)	46.4%
Private clients	9.0%
Institutional investors	16.4%
Banks (including Euroclear)	28.2%

Source: *Annual Report*
Note: *assets are defined as account, fiduciary and securities assets; for banks, only securities assets*

Portfolio management demands a hi-tech capability, and SBC's introduction of their Portfolio Management Decision Support system is claimed to be state-of-the-art, using modern portfolio theory to facilitate asset allocation and streamline administration.

Investment funds have been extended by the bank as part of the private banking and private client focus, and assets of Swiss- and Luxembourg-based investment funds increased by 45.9 per cent to SFr49.6 billion in 1993. Some 55 additional investment funds, with assets of SFr2.4 billion, are managed by subsidiaries and foreign branches. A new collaboration with the Zurich Insurance Group, and with the inclusion of BSI since January 1994, brought in premiums valued at SFr110 million.

Table A4.2 SBC investment funds

	End 1993 SFrm	Fund assets change %	Net in/outflow SFrm
Asset allocation funds	3,154.4	463.1	2,435.9
Money market and short-term funds	21,485.9	19.5	2,706.3
Bond funds	16,135.2	51.7	4,637.7
Equity funds	5,867.1	205.0	2,743.6
Property funds	2,983.9	2.7	
Overall total	49,626.5		12,523.4

Source: *Annual Reports*, Business Interventions

SBC's commission income (net) was SFr2.6 billion in 1993, an increase of 27.5 per cent, largely contributed by the private banking group in Switzerland, the Luxembourg operation and securities trading in Asia. Fees from asset management services also grew by 36.1 per cent, although custodian fees showed only a moderate growth. Lower interest rates led to a drop in investment, and thus commissions from fiduciary transactions decreased by just under SFr1 billion, a 2.9 per cent decrease. In 1992, commission income from investment and administration activities accounted for 51 per cent, while loan commissions were 15.3 per cent and brokerage, syndication and placement fees were 33.7 per cent.

In Switzerland, the Private Banking Group reported consolidated operating income of SFr598 million (after interest and commissions paid); with an operating expenditure of SFr371 million, the annual profit for the group was SFr82 million. BSI (Banca della Suizzera Italiana) showed a gross profit of SFr155 million, and the other companies in the group boosted commission income, particularly from securities and investment business. Private banking and trust services in the Channel Islands increased assets by 16.7 per cent, with profit of £2.1 million; Luxembourg saw gross operating profit after tax up 34.6 per cent to LFr2.2 billion. In Monaco, where the Banque de Placements et de Crédit was renamed as Société de Banque Suisse (Monaco), one saw customer deposits drop by 2.9 per cent as low interest rates encouraged shifts out of time deposits into securities. Nassau profits were $5.1 million, and Grand Cayman climbed 45 per cent to $11.7 million; in Panama impressive profit growth of 78.1 per cent brought in $6.8 million.

Crédit Suisse

The private banking operation of Crédit Suisse is complex, in that some services are offered through Leu Holding, and some through the overall Crédit Suisse name; both entities are part of the CS Holding Group. Services include investment advisory (which covers current accounts, deposits, fixed income, equities, foreign exchange, precious metals and derivative products); portfolio management (for balanced portfolio, fixed income portfolio, equity portfolio, ForeX trading, precious metals, cross-currency leverage); financial products, which capitalise on Allfinanz services within the overall CS Holding Group; and offshore trust services.

Leu Holding became part of Crédit Suisse following a hostile bid in 1990. At that time, Bank Leu was the fifth largest in Switzerland, but net profits had plunged from SFr53m to only SFr3m after a poor year in securities trading, and SFr61m provision against liabilities arising out of substantial fraud at a branch office. The bank had a top quality client list, and fee earning activities accounted for around 30 per cent of all income; fiduciary business was increased over 1989–90.

CS Holding holds 53.9 per cent of Leu Holding, which in turn comprises 11 subsidiaries: these include Bank Leu, Bank Hofmann, Clariden Bank, Bank Heusser & Co. and Fundus & Treuhand.

Over the last five years, Crédit Suisse has been strengthening its overseas operations: it was the first Swiss bank to open a branch in Italy, based on an acquisition from the Bank of New York, and has been concentrating on corporate business and building up the private banking side. In addition, links have been made within Central and Eastern Europe, with representative offices in Vienna and Moscow, and an expanding private banking operation in the US. At the end of 1990, a majority interest was acquired in BEA Associates Inc., to serve as the bank's asset management focus for US tax-exempt pension institutions, and since then new private banking operations have been opened in Miami and Los Angeles.

In 1992, the bank saw an improvement in the yield curve of customer deposits, when sight deposits were up by SFr0.7 billion (6.4 per cent) to SFr12 billion. Time deposits showed another year-on-year increase, rising by SFr4.7 billion, or 7.8 per cent, to reach SFr65.6 billion. This remained the largest customer deposit category, accounting for 40 per cent of total assets. Deposits held in savings and investment savings accounts for the year increased to SFr15.3 billion, partly due to the takeover of the EKO Bank and Gewerbebank Baden. With the introduction of the new Crédit Suisse Private Banking service, the bank developed investment and financial counselling services, and built the international presence by expanding foreign-based investment and portfolio management units. German and UK asset management services were expanded through SKA Trust GmbH and SKA Investment GmbH, in Frankfurt, and through Crédit Suisse Asset Management Ltd in London. The latter had a particularly successful 1992 with short-term corporate portfolios focused on money market products.

Most Crédit Suisse investment funds are registered in Luxembourg, a change from the mid-1980s, when 92 per cent of them were Swiss-registered and 8 per cent in Luxembourg. At the end of 1992, 64 per cent were lodged under Luxembourg law, and it is likely that this will continue to be the case after the 'no' vote on the EEA. Total net assets held in Crédit Suisse funds rose by 40 per cent in 1992, to more than SFr25 billion; star performers were Money Market Funds, and the addition of two high-yielding currencies – the peseta and the Belgian franc – was popular. A new expert computer system, CS Fondex, was introduced during the year to formulate combinations of fund units for individual investors.

Commission income in 1992 was SFr1.6 billion, based on investment business, securities administration and commercial activities. Consolidated income from on-balance-sheet activities held steady at around the 1991 level, coping with the sharp rise in provisions against non-performing loans. For 1993, Crédit Suisse reported a 53 per cent rise in consolidated net income to SFr1.46 billion, despite an 81 per cent jump in loss provisions to SFr 2.8 billion.

The acquisition of Swiss Volksbank in 1993 distorts the figures, but it is clear that gains in income have been made from trading and services, more than offsetting depressed interest income and the cost of bad loans. Commission income, mainly from asset management, rose sharply by 54 per cent to SFr2.6 billion, and interest income was up 20 per cent to SFr2.8 billion, due to the consolidation of Volksbank. Profit before taxes and provisions increased 62 per cent to SFr4.6 billion. Total Crédit Suisse assets at the year end were up 34 per cent to SFr232 billion.

Crédit Suisse has a considerable international operation, and leverages its internal corporate finance and trading activities to the advantage of private clients; CS First Boston, the investment bank, is more than 75 per cent owned by CS Holding, which has the intention of gaining outright ownership. Private banking activities have received considerable focus in the last two years. Cultural changes have been necessary, with more focus being placed on relationship officers actively seeking greater business from existing clients, and referrals for new business – a very non-Swiss attitude. Described by a senior executive as the ability to 'dare asking', this change in the marketing approach reflects the bank's appreciation of the need fully to understand client needs, in a global context. Asking for referral also gives immediate feedback as to the level of comfort and satisfaction the client has with the bank's services.

For many years the universal banks, Crédit Suisse among them, have waited for business to come their way in a rather passive manner. Current climate demands that private bank officers go out into the world with, and for, their clients, and act in a more fully developed partnership. The bank has also recognised the need to go after new money, with all the attendant sophistication and expectation that requires. Focus areas for development include Latin America, Italy and Southern Europe. Asia Pacific is also providing significant business growth.

UBS

UBS is the largest, most profitable and most highly capitalised of the Swiss Big Three banks, and has triple A credit rating. Foreign assets accounted for 55 per cent of the balance sheet total in 1990. In the 1980s, the bank's focus was on international investment banking: the growth potential for this in Switzerland was limited by its already strong market share and the competitive marketplace. Its purchase of Phillips & Drew (now UBS Securities) took $100 million, even after considerable losses between the crash of 1987 and the end of 1988. New decisions and strategy led to securities operations being merged into a single unit; fund management became a separate subsidiary, and private banking was kept in the branches. UBS had a strong ForeX market share in London and the Far East, with a merchant banking operation in Milan, 20 per cent market share of securities trading volume in Switzerland, and 35 per cent of SOFFEX traded volume. It also had the dominant position in fund management, a crucial weapon in the private banker's armoury: as the largest fund manager, it had private banking subsidiaries in Tokyo, London, Frankfurt and in Singapore, through CANTrade.

Development of the London private banking operation has been the brainchild of Peter Braunwalder, formerly an investment banker in Japan. He and Rudi Mueller set up the private banking operation in London, and the attractions of London's international reputation for performance driven asset management in combination with UBS's stature has brought the private bank swift growth. A four-year plan was formulated in 1990, sanctioned by the group management board. In 1993, UBS had tripled its private banking business, though only midway through its four-year investment plan; consolidation in 1994 was expected to be followed by growth in 1995. Ambitious growth is achieved through referral, and asking for referral, which is largely successful given the UBS name and position in the market overall. Investment advisors work on the American investment bank approach, calling clients and presenting opportunities; marketeers make the customer acquisition and manage client relationships.

The London client base tends to be wholesale, with a lot of $1m accounts, and there are also many HINWIs who demand the most sophisticated attention and performance, perhaps through leverage of other trading and investment activities with UBS. These clients are more likely to have between $3 and $6 million in assets. In comparing private clients with, for example, pension fund management, UBS is careful to point out that institutional money managers have indices and benchmarking measures with which to make comparisons; the private client, in contrast, may not be well served by such measures, since in general the trend is towards absolute return rather than a relative one. Around 35 per cent of UBS private clients have discretionary portfolio management, with a further 40 per cent taking advisory services. Entrepreneurs are more inclined to move their accounts after a couple of years, but large accounts are rarely moved, according to the bank.

Discretionary management services are available to clients with a minimum of £500k to invest, based on discussion of investment objectives and attitudes to risk-taking. Time horizons and tax efficiency are also carefully factored into investment advice. Advisory services are provided to clients with a lower asset balance. Portfolio types include income or capital growth orientated balanced portfolios; cash management funds investing in money market instruments; fixed income funds including both bonds and cash; pure equity funds; and special products including derivatives.

UBS draws attention, somewhat unusually for a private bank, to collateral loans in its promotional literature. This offers clients a means of gearing up their portfolio, and is not foreign to other banks, who use the Lombard credit approach, perhaps less overtly. The London private bank operates autonomously within the overall UBS group, and leverages its integration of trading and investment activities in the Broadgate office.

Off-balance-sheet business continued to provide significant returns for the bank in 1993, with the total volume of derivative products amounting to SFr2 billion at the end of the first six months. In 1992, services income for investment counselling and asset management operations amounted to SFr 2.4 billion, an increase of 16.1 per cent and SFr337 million over the previous year. Including international credit, issuing operations and corporate finance, the net income from services was SFr3.1 billion. Fiduciary operations total was SFr43.6 billion, down 18.2 per cent from SFr53.3 billion.

Like the other Swiss banks, UBS saw tremendous growth in investment funds, of which the largest contribution was made by Luxembourg-based funds. Their assets soared by nearly 50 per cent to SFr21.9 billion, and money market funds accounted for a significant portion of this growth. Total assets of all UBS investment funds rose by 34 per cent to SFr33.6 billion, and the number of funds was expanded to 59, with the launch of three new ones in Luxembourg.

UK BANKS: REINVENTING A TRADITIONAL MARKET

Coutts & Co./Coutts & Co. International Private Banking

The cachet of the Coutts name, as the 'royal' bank, is a major asset in the private bank business. The 300-year-old bank underwent significant reorganisation between 1991 and 1993, leading to the establishment of Coutts & Co. International Private Banking, and bringing together various entities outside the UK which contributed to the international private banking operations of the Coutts Group. It is wholly owned by NatWest Bank, and David Went, Chief Executive of NatWest's Ulster Bank subsidiary, was appointed in April 1994 to the new post of Chief Executive of Coutts Group. The Group is parent of Coutts & Co. in the UK, and in 1994–95, the international and UK private banking operations were consolidated into a single entity. The bank plans to build a world-class private banking operation to rival J. P. Morgan and Citicorp.

Results for the international bank in 1992 showed a 20 per cent growth in client assets under administration, which generated similar growth in income streams; operating profits were up 40 per cent. A strong programme to minimise costs, helped by the merging of business entities and thus the potential for rationalisation, saw a reduction in staff numbers of 6 per cent.

The bank's focus on marketing in 1992 majored on improved client segmentation and the development of new country marketing plans. A high proportion of the international business is in asset management, and emphasis was placed on widening the product range and improving service delivery. A much-vaunted MIS system and improved telecommunications allowed the bank to gauge client requirements more accurately, and also both product and client profitability. Investment in upgrading the skills and professionalism of the investment management capability, and continuous development of offshore trust and asset protection activities contributed to the provision of a comprehensive cross-border wealth management package.

In the UK, 1992 saw a return to profit after a low point in 1991; a net profit figure of £2.9 million before tax was achieved. Continuing high levels of provisions for bad debts, restructuring costs and other exceptional items disguised the improvements at the operating level. Cost reduction in 1992 achieved substantial savings. An increase in income of 8 per cent came largely from fee income, which in itself grew by nearly 20 per cent. Fee-earning services continued to be a focus area for 1993, and the jump in profits of £29.8 million reflected this emphasis. Total revenues were up by £6.5 million to £129.8 million, and the profit increase was some 24 per cent.

Coutts UK operation is somewhat different to other private banks', and has been described as 'red-carpet retail'; this is reflected in the weak demand for retail lending, as in the retail sector overall, and record business in mortgages.

Market segmentation continued in the UK, with the intention of matching resources to the differing demands of individual clients. Two new offices opened during the year, and an Overseas Client Office was established in London, specialising in providing UK banking services for individuals temporarily resident in the UK, and the internationally mobile; this service continued to be successful, and provided an increase in introductions to the international arm. Competition in private banking in the UK grew during the year, with further new entrants – and more to come throughout the decade.

International results showed a 20 per cent increase in total income, to £156 million; the corporate loan book was substantially reduced, and so therefore was the balance sheet. Commission income grew by 30 per cent, and after two years of flat costs, considerable investment went into building future potential; operating costs grew by 9 per cent. Client assets under administration total more than £17 billion, on fully discretionary, advisory and custodial bases. The New York office was upgraded to branch status, and has 50 staff; in Miami a dramatic growth in assets under management led to increased staff numbers, and trust capabilities were enhanced by the opening of Coutts & Co. Bermuda. Plans in 1994 included opening offices in Cannes, Athens, Los Angeles and Buenos Aires.

During 1993 the number of umbrella UCITS funds was expanded from 4 to 24, and there was a 150 per cent increase in placements into these funds. Emerging markets emphasis has seen the creation of specifically Latin American funds.

Kleinwort Benson

Kleinwort Benson Private Bank has offices in London, the Channel Islands and Geneva, as well as in Vienna, Brussels, Paris, Frankfurt and Madrid. The bank suffered in the UK in 1992, when profitability deteriorated. Investment management and private banking saw a drop from £24.4m in 1991 to £22.1m over the year. Kleinwort Benson attributed this to an increase in mortgage lending provisions for doubtful debts, an indication of the problems associated with private banking when activities cover both investment and credit. (The US style of private banking, which incorporates credit as a key factor in gaining and growing wealthy individuals as clients, has suffered similarly.) Kleinwort's strategy is to continue expanding its lending business, concentrating on clients who are already, or appear likely to become, interested in the overall private banking business.

The bank was helped by an inflow of private client assets for portfolio management, which provided growth in advisory services. Jersey and Guernsey operations met objectives for client satisfaction and profitability, expanding their range of offshore corporate services and clients, and an improvement in profitability was seen in the Geneva private banking operation. UK clients for the offshore business are largely expatriate, and the bank's Channel Island operation has seen significant growth – to the extent that in 1993 it was worth more than the overall operation's market evaluation two years earlier. Out of a total of KB's 2,700 staff, 450 of them are Channel Island based.

A survey of private portfolio management clients drew a strong response, and has been pivotal in the development of services. Changes in team approach and continued emphasis on service, rather than product, are viewed as key; the emphasis on continuity of relationships is described in their phrase, 'Our people grow grey with their clients.'

Interim figures for 1993 showed investment management, including private banking, standing at £10.6m, an exact match for the same six months in 1992. Client assets under management rose in value from £9.8 billion to £10.8 billion in 1992, and assets under administration increased to £2.6 billion.

Clients are segmented and analysed according to interest, for example media or entertainment. Marketing is largely through referral, with some effort going into the development of relationships with professionals. Service development is driven via the intermediary sales force, independent audit and market research, and focus groups. Client acquisition is likely to cost the best part of first year earnings.

Established in 1792 as a merchant bank, Kleinwort Benson's private banking business incorporates a full range of services and products, including high interest cheque accounts. Managing director George Alford foresees a competitive battleground for the 'trainee wealthy', clients who are between 30 and 45, and much competition from stockbrokers and other non-traditional private bankers. The bank views the question of identity as crucial to success over the next five years, along with recognition that it is the client driving the business. Within that context, banks will then compete on price via product. However there is some concern that the industry is in oversupply, with people who rush into the market and push the pricing down: in KB's view, pricing is properly done against service delivery, with higher fees for higher levels of service.

The bank's activities in the fund management field have been growing over the last two years. This provides a potential growth route for private banking clients. New ventures include emerging market funds, and a joint venture with the Indian Tata Group, to establish a new fund management company in the sub-continent. It estimates that economic reform in the domestic Indian market – primarily the middle class population – is producing an increase in the number of new retail investors of between two and three million people per year who are increasingly turning to the capital markets.

Like many other private banking operations, Kleinwort has a highly developed institutional business, associated of course with its merchant banking origins. The bank benefits from Treasury and dealing services in-house, facilitating client business and management of the private bank Treasury positions. Managed trusts are a key development area for both institutional and private investors.

APPENDIX 4

Newer entrants to the UK market

The interest in private banking in the UK market has been growing over the last decade, spurred on during the boom years of the 1980s and recognition by the larger retail banks that this is a good and profitable business to be in. Thus Lloyds Private Bank was born; Barclays, which had an international private banking operation in Switzerland, has consolidated its focus over the last three years; and the Midland, as part of HSBC, has a young international business, with plans to develop its UK presence in 1994 and thereafter.

INDEX